Reshaping America's Military

Four Alternatives
Presented as
Presidential Speeches

Lawrence J. Korb, Project Director

A Council Policy Initiative

Sponsored by the Council on Foreign Relations

Founded in 1921, the Council on Foreign Relations is a nonpartisan membership organi-zation, research center, and publisher. It is dedicated to increasing America's understand-ing of the world and contributing ideas to U.S. foreign policy. The Council accomplishes this mainly by promoting constructive discussions and by publishing *Foreign Affairs*, the leading journal on global issues. The Council is host to the widest possible range of views, but an advocate of none, though its research fellows and Independent Task Forces do take policy stands.

THE COUNCIL TAKES NO INSTITUTIONAL POSITION ON POLICY ISSUES AND HAS NO AFFILIATION WITH THE U.S. GOVERNMENT. ALL STATE-MENTS OF FACT AND EXPRESSIONS OF OPINION CONTAINED IN ALL ITS PUBLICATIONS ARE THE SOLE RESPONSIBILITY OF THE AUTHOR OR AUTHORS.

This volume is the fifth in a series of Council on Foreign Relations Policy Initiatives (CPIs) designed to encourage debate among interested Americans on crucial foreign policy top-ics by presenting the issues and policy choices in terms easily understood by experts and nonexperts alike. The substance of the volume benefited from the comments of several ana-lysts and many reviewers, but responsibility for the final text remains with the project direc-tor and the authors.

Other Council Policy Initiatives:

Humanitarian Intervention (2000), Alton Frye, Project Director; *Future Visions for U.S. Defense Policy* (1998; revised, 2000), John Hillen and Lawrence Korb, Project Directors; *Toward an International Criminal Court* (1999), Alton Frye, Project Director; *Future Visions for U.S. Trade Policy* (1998), Bruce Stokes, Project Director.

Council on Foreign Relations Books, Task Force Reports, and CPIs are distributed by Brook-ings Institution Press (1-800-275-1447). For further information about the Council or this paper, please write the Council on Foreign Relations, 58 East 68th Street, New York, NY 10021, or call the Director of Communications at 212-434-9400. Visit our website at www.cfr.org.

CONTENTS

Foreword   v

Acknowledgments   vii

Memorandum to the President   1

   Table 1: U.S. Defense Policy Reviews   25

   Table 2: International Comparison of Defense
      Spending   26

Speech One: An Enhanced Defense   27

Speech Two: A Revolutionary Transformation   44

Speech Three: An Evolutionary Transformation   62

Speech Four: A Cooperative Defense   77

Figures

  1. Defense Spending as a Share of GDP, 1960–2007   94

  2. Defense Spending as a Share of Federal Outlays,
     1945–2007   94

  3. Department of Defense Annual Budget Authority,
     1945–2003   95

  4. Federal Budget Requests, FY2003   95

  5. Department of Defense Budget by Service,
     1980–2003   96

  6. Makeup of Department of Defense Budget, FY2003   96

FOREWORD

The purpose of this Council Policy Initiative (CPI), as with the others we have produced since 1997, is to promote a debate among interested Americans on key international issues. We foster this debate by providing background information on a given subject and drafting speeches that the U.S. president might deliver, each making the best case for a plausible policy option on the issue.

In this CPI we lay out four possible approaches to dealing with the new lineup of threats to U.S. national security.

1) *Enhanced defense:* The United States is the sole superpower in the world and must substantially increase spending on both existing and future capabilities. We must do this in order to ensure the country's capability to deal with both traditional (and symmetrical) and non-traditional (or asymmetrical) threats, such as those that were horribly realized on September 11, 2001.

2) *Revolutionary transformation:* The most serious threats to U.S. security lie in the future. Since it takes so long to bring weapons into the field, however, we must begin making heavy investments in revolutionary technologies now to ensure we can meet those threats when they arise. In the meantime, we have enough residual military capability to defend against the threats we need worry about at present.

3) *Evolutionary transformation:* Serious threats to U.S. security exist here and now, and we must rebuild our existing capability to combat them; meanwhile, and secondarily, we can continue to invest in future technology as we have for the past decade. The soundness of this evolutionary approach was demonstrated in the war against the Taliban and al Qaeda in Afghanistan. The brilliant results achieved by U.S. forces demonstrated that no radical revolution is needed.

4) *Cooperative defense:* The United States cannot and should not attempt to meet the array of existing threats by itself, but

should cooperate with its allies and help build international institutions to share the necessary security responsibilities.

This CPI has been revised to reflect both the fallout of the September 11 attacks and the fiscal year 2003–07 defense program, which was submitted to Congress on February 4, 2002.

I would like to thank the primary author of this CPI, Larry Korb, Vice President and Director of the Council's Studies Department, for spearheading this effort. Although this publication is called a Council Policy Initiative, it really was Larry's initiative and brainwork that made it come to life.

Leslie H. Gelb
President, Council on Foreign Relations

ACKNOWLEDGMENTS

This Council Policy Initiative could not have been completed without the efforts and contributions of several people.

The Project Director would like to thank first and foremost, Alexandre Tiersky, a Research Associate in the Studies Department, who conducted research, typed the manuscripts, prepared the tables, and made several helpful contributions to the text itself; Patricia Dorff, Kim Fielding, and Celia Whitaker, who did a superb job of editing the text; Sameen Gauhar, who edited and graciously carried the CPI through the final haul; John Hillen, who, as the Council's Olin Fellow for National Security in 1997, served as Project Director for an earlier version of this initiative; and Andrew Bacevich of Boston University, Marcus Corbin of the Center for Defence Information, Dan Koslofsky of the Council for a Livable World, and Michael O'Hanlon of the Brookings Institution for commenting on the drafts.

We are grateful for the generous support of the Carnegie Corporation of New York, without which the project would not have been possible.

MEMORANDUM TO THE PRESIDENT

FROM: "The National Security Adviser"

SUBJECT: U.S. Military Responses to the New Lineup of Threats; Alternative Defense Policy Speeches

PURPOSE

As you submit your first five-year defense program to Congress and the country, it is essential that you develop a defense policy that conforms to the new and changing threats to U.S. national security and prepare a realistic and affordable strategy for dealing with them. The events of September 11 make this is an incredibly important undertaking.

You have wisely launched a serious debate about reformulating U.S. defense policy in the wake of September 11, in particular with the defense spending increases you proposed. Noticeably absent from this debate, however, has been an overarching discussion of the principles behind your budgets and the implementation of your plans.

To contribute to a well-reasoned analysis and an in-depth discussion of all the possibilities available to you at this critical juncture, we present the following memorandum. It is designed to make the best cases for four plausible defense policies, providing background information and a comparative analysis of each one. The memo is followed by four speeches that each present a clear strategic thrust. Here are the four specific options:

Enhanced Defense: The United States is the sole superpower in the world and must substantially increase spending on both existing and future capabilities in order to ensure we have the wherewithal to match our expansive interests. As the events of September 11 demonstrated, those who predicted that the end of the Cold War meant the end of threats to our security interests at home and abroad were wrong.

America's unique superpower status brings with it a unique burden for the U.S. armed forces. They must be ready to meet a full range of threats—from conventional war among major powers to attacks by terrorists with global reach—and also be prepared to participate in peacekeeping operations. The problem is that the military's capability and readiness have diminished over the last decade, as defense spending has declined in real terms to less than 3 percent of GDP. We must therefore upgrade our military superiority almost across the board, with resources more or less evenly divided among the services. In addition to making some technological advances, we will also need to rely more on allies for peacekeeping duties. Over the course of the next few years, we will increase the share of GDP spent on defense to 4 percent, adding roughly $100 billion a year to military spending—enough to fund existing force levels, raise the quality of life for the men and women in the armed services to acceptable standards, pay for a higher level of procurement, and invest in vital new technologies.

Mr. President, this course is favored by the secretary of defense, the Joint Chiefs of Staff, and many conservatives in both parties, and it is closest to what you have advocated since the events of September 11.

Revolutionary Transformation: The most serious challenges to American military power lie in the future. As the war in Afghanistan demonstrated, the United States currently enjoys overwhelming military power sufficient to defeat any adversary on the traditional battlefield. Since it takes so long to bring weapons into the field, however, we must immediately begin making heavy investments in revolutionary technologies to ensure that we can defeat potential future adversaries; in the meantime, the military capability we have is sufficient to defend against the few military threats we need worry about at present.

If we take advantage of the opportunities presented by remarkable advances in both information technology and long-range warfighting capabilities—which together have been called a "revolution in military affairs"—no enemy will be able to challenge us in this century. In embracing this revolutionary transformation, we will shift our focus from Europe to Asia, move beyond the strategy of preparing for two "major regional conflicts" (MRCs), and concentrate our efforts on developing next-generation weapons systems. We will provide our forces with information superiority, safety through stealth, superior striking speed, agility and mobility, and the capability to operate in a truly joint fashion. We will also break free from an offense-dominated strategic posture by deploying missile defenses and making significant cuts in our nuclear arsenal. Finally, we will alter the proportions of the defense budget allocated to each service, which have remained fixed for the past 20 years, by boosting the share of the Air Force relative to that of the Army and Navy.

Mr. President, this option is closest to the program you outlined in your campaign and were pursuing until the events of September 11. It is supported by many defense experts in Congress as well as defense intellectuals.

Evolutionary Transformation: As the events of September 11 demonstrated, the United States faces serious threats to its security here and now. We must rebuild the existing capability to combat them; meanwhile, and secondarily, we can continue to invest in future technology as we have for the past decade.

The war in Afghanistan demonstrated that radical overhauls at the Pentagon are neither necessary nor truly possible. Although investing in new technology is always important, the United States cannot afford to completely ignore current security threats from terrorists with global reach or in places like Iraq, the Korean Peninsula, and the Taiwan Straits. A decade of underfunding has left many of the military's weapons, vehicles, aircraft, and support systems near to—or already at—block obsolescence. The United States must rectify that situation so it can be prepared to address numerous near-term challenges, even as it innovates and modernizes. Some change at the Pentagon would be useful: for instance, the services' shares of the defense budget need to be altered somewhat, and the military can probably make do with a slightly smaller force structure and fewer legacy (or traditional) weapons systems, like the Crusader, than are currently planned. And although we should continue to pursue vigorous research and development in the area of missile defense, funding unproven technology should not come before putting our military back on its feet.

Mr. President, this course is favored by a majority of the Democrats in Congress and by most of our allies.

Cooperative Defense: The war against terrorism clearly shows that the United States cannot and should not attempt to meet the array of existing threats by itself. Instead, we should cooperate with our allies and help build international institutions to share the necessary security responsibilities. If we do not work with our allies on military matters, we cannot expect them to cooperate with us in other areas important to our security such as getting better intelligence about possible terrorist activities, drying up financial flows to terrorist groups, and bringing terrorists to justice.

By keeping military spending at or near Cold War levels and continuing to assume unilateral responsibility and leadership during most cases of international turmoil, we are going to overload domestic circuits and, as you saw in your trips to the NATO summit in May 2001 and to Europe in May 2002, may alienate European allies by widening the technology gap between our military and theirs. We may also aggravate the grievances that serve as rallying points for those who fan the flames of anti-Americanism and thus potentially worsen the terrorist problem. Moreover, we will not be able to solve the gravest threats to our security—global problems such as terrorism, drugs, disease, and the proliferation of weapons of mass destruction (WMD).

True security will not come from simply maintaining U.S. military capabilities: now is the time when we must also support international agreements on security-related matters and help build international institutions and ad hoc collective security coalitions. The United States and our friends and allies need these new arrangements to focus on a new threat: failed states that can serve as breeding grounds for terrorists. Building these new layers of cooperation will take time, so we should begin now; every step should be carefully coordinated with our allies, particularly those in the Muslim world.

An additional benefit of this approach is that we can eventually reduce military spending by 15 to 20 percent by ridding ourselves of a wasteful and cumbersome military that is still shaped too much by Cold War thinking. We can use those funds where they are most needed—in the war against terrorism—and in particular to support agencies such as the Coast Guard, FBI, CIA, and Immigration and Naturalization Service (INS).

Mr. President, this option is supported by traditional internationalists in Congress and the arms-control community.

Mr. President, we give you speeches that each lay out one of the above options, so you can get a feel for making the case to the public. Although the speeches are not written for experts, they are written by experts, so you and your speechwriters would certainly need to polish the presentation. Each speech is also purely focused on one particular direction. The aim of the purity is to clarify your choices. Obviously, in an actual speech you could mix, match, and blend the choices somewhat. The speeches address what a defense policy must consider: namely, what kinds of forces we should develop to meet likely military threats and support U.S. engagement and leadership in the international system.

Finally, it is important to note that these speeches do not directly discuss plans to bolster homeland security. They are focused primarily on what shape our military must take in order to best respond to the threats they will face. The homeland security mission will involve the military but not in a central role. We therefore have not focused directly on that issue in these speeches.

BACKGROUND

After a decade of ad hoc policymaking, the United States after September 11 has an extraordinary opportunity—and responsibility—to undertake a fundamental review of its national security strategy and defense policy. An entire new category of threats became terrifyingly real last fall, and although our armed forces performed admirably in Afghanistan, we still need to work out the organizing principles on which the military should be structured and funded. Now is an opportune moment to do so, because in 2002, America faces no readily apparent major conventional military threats or likely strategic nuclear threats (although the rusting Russian nuclear arsenal is a concern).

Terrorism is not the only dangerous challenge for which our military must plan: rogue states such as Iraq, Iran, and North Korea, which you described as constituting an "axis of evil" in your January 2002 State of the Union speech, continue to be of concern. A host of emerging security threats such as ethnic violence and refugee problems in failed or failing states, and the possibility of new forms of warfare, continue to give our military planners headaches. You made clear during the presidential campaign that your awareness of this new environment, coupled with the Quadrennial Defense Review (QDR) that your Defense Department completed in the fall of 2001, would lead your administration to undertake a serious reexamination of U.S. defense strategy, force size and structure, weapons systems, overseas deployments, and the organization and workings of the Department of Defense (DoD).

Since 1991, DoD has completed four major defense policy reviews to address these questions: the Joint Chiefs of Staff-led Base Force Review (1991), the Clinton administration's Bottom-Up Review (1993), and the first and second congressionally mandated QDR (1997 and 2001). In addition, three independent panels established by Congress have undertaken comprehensive examinations of DoD's budget, force structure, strategy, deployment posture, and modernization program: the 1994–95 Commission on Roles and Missions of the Armed Forces, the 1997 National Defense Panel (NDP), and the 1998 National Security Strategy Group, which completed its work in early 2001.

As shown in Table 1, the internal DoD reviews generally produced few changes, aside from matching smaller (but similar) force structures to a defense spending account that declined nearly 30 percent between 1989 and 1997, leveled off, and then increased slightly in real terms in the last four years and will increase dramatically in 2002 and for the foreseeable future. In the absence of a clear strategy, such as that of the Cold War's containment policy, DoD has done little beyond these "budget drills" to define the purposes and strategy of U.S. military forces.

[6]

Moreover, there has been no shortage of recent security challenges that we have used the U.S. military to counter. Before the current deployment in Afghanistan and the Philippines, U.S. forces have been frequently deployed in the past ten years for missions ranging from traditional deterrence and war fighting (the Korean Peninsula, Kuwait) to humanitarian relief and peacekeeping operations (Somalia, Haiti, Bosnia, Rwanda, Kosovo). You pointed out in your speech at the Citadel in September 1999 that U.S. forces had been used for unexpected contingency operations almost once every nine weeks in the previous nine years. In addition, threats such as terrorism, the proliferation of WMD and ballistic missile technology, international crime, and other global problems pose new challenges to American security to which military forces may be part of an appropriate response.

The 1991 Base Force Review and the 1993 Bottom-Up Review both postulated that the United States should make combat readiness its priority and focus on preparing for MRCs, such as those that might occur on the Korean Peninsula or in the Persian Gulf. These reviews were heavily criticized for being excessively focused on near-term contingencies at the expense of long-term preparedness and modernization and for overestimating the potency of the threats in these regions at the expense of other conventional challenges. They also came under fire for failing to adequately fund the force necessary to carry out a two-MRC strategy, according to the Joint Chiefs of Staff's estimations. Some of the criticism was vindicated in the following years when, between 1993 and 1997, the U.S. military found its greatest challenges outside the MRC contingencies—in multilateral interventions to aid troubled states such as Somalia, Haiti, and Bosnia.

Congress mandated the 1997 QDR to connect DoD strategy and funding more closely to threats in the post–Cold War world. The QDR report, released in May 1997, kept the basic two-MRC strategy intact, added the need for DoD to prepare for and perform "smaller-scale contingencies" (SSCs), such as the operation in Bosnia, and cut the total force by an additional 115,000 uniformed personnel while maintaining basically the same force structure. Congress also put together the independent National Defense Panel to critique the QDR, selecting for the panel former civilian and military officials (some of whom are now part of your national security team). The NDP provided an initial memorandum to the president that included an assessment of the review. Their analysis was damning on many fronts. It argued that the QDR focused too much on the near term (the next five to ten years), maintained the two-MRC strategy without adequate justification, added missions and cut spending without setting mission priorities, failed to connect strategy with programs and budgets, ignored some important strategic developments (such as the role of outer space), and paid little attention to allies and coalitions. The National Security Strategy Group echoed many of these comments.

The NDP report, released in December 1997, did not specifically identify the principal military challenges of 2020 and beyond. It did not "attempt to provide all the answers." Rather, its aim was to "stimulate a wider debate on our defense priorities." The panel recommended the "accelerat[ion]" of a "transformation strategy" aimed at military and national security structures, operational concepts and equipment, and key DoD business processes. Specifically, the NDP identified new operational challenges likely to confront U.S. forces, such as the absence of access to forward bases, information attacks (e.g., a strike against U.S. computer or communications systems), war in outer space, deep inland operations, urban operations, and new forms of attacks against the U.S. homeland itself. It criticized the amount of money planned for upgrading older weapon systems and suggested that the military exploit innovative new technologies by designing and purchasing new weapons that emphasize stealth, speed, mobility, precision-strike capability, and advanced automation. Under pressure from the Joint Chiefs of Staff, the secretary of defense rejected the recommendations of the panel. But you used the NDP's report as a template for your September 1999 speech at the Citadel.

The U.S. Commission on National Security/21st Century, better known as the Hart-Rudman Commission, after Co-Chairmen and former U.S. Senators Gary Hart (D-Colo.) and Warren Rudman (R-N.H.), issued its "Road Map for National Security: Imperative for Change" in March 2001. This report argued that the two-war criterion failed to generate armed forces strong enough to meet the real challenges facing the nation.

[8]

Moreover, the report argued, current levels of defense spending were adequate to meet the demands now placed on the U.S. military and those anticipated in the upcoming 25 years. The commission recommended increased attention to defending the homeland—asserting that "a direct attack against American citizens on American soil is likely over the next quarter century"—and guaranteeing access to outer space. Further, the commission advocated doubling the federal research and development budget by 2010 to "recapitalize America's strengths in science and education." To that end, it recommended reforming the foreign policy apparatus of the executive branch to clarify the process of policy formulation; deploying five kinds of military forces, from strategic-nuclear forces to homeland security, conventional, expeditionary, and humanitarian/constabulary forces; and adapting "alliances and other regional mechanisms to a new era in which America's partners seek greater autonomy and responsibility." The commission's conclusions, particularly about homeland defense, have acquired particular relevance now that terrorists have inflicted massive casualties on the United States.

Your own administration's QDR, which was completed before the September 11 attacks and released on September 30, 2001, attempted to answer some of the criticisms of these outside panels. It sets out three new directions for U.S. defense strategy.

First, we decided to move away from the two MRC force-sizing construct, which called for maintaining forces capable of simultaneously marching on and occupying the capitals of two adversaries and changing their regimes. The new approach instead places greater emphasis on deterrence in four critical theaters, backed by the ability to swiftly defeat two aggressors at the same time, while preserving the option for one major offensive to occupy an aggressor's capital and replace the regime. By removing the requirement to maintain a second occupation force, we can free up resources both for various, lesser contingencies that might face us and also for investment in the future.

Second, to confront a world marked by surprise and substantial uncertainty, we agreed to shift our planning from the "threat-based" model that has guided our thinking in the past to a "capabilities-based" model. We do not know who may threaten us or when or where. But we do have some sense of what they may threaten us with and how. We also have a sense of what capabilities can provide us important new advantages against our enemies.

Third, this capabilities-based approach places great emphasis on defining where we want to go with the transformation of our forces. Transformation, as Secretary of Defense Donald Rumsfeld has said, "is about an awful lot more than bombs and bullets and dollars and cents; it's about new approaches, it's about culture, it's about mindset and ways of thinking of things."

Since 1998, more than $200 billion has been added to the five-year defense program. But the bulk of this funding has gone to improving the quality of life and readiness of existing forces. Thus, more than a decade after the end of the Cold War and after several major policy reviews—and as we look toward a protracted "war on terror" with no foreseeable endpoint, in which our military will play a central role—several important questions about U.S. defense policy remain unanswered: How central a role will our armed forces play in the "war on terror," and how will these new priorities stack up with their pre-September 11 missions? What weapons, strategies, and forces will be necessary for these new priorities? Should DoD resources be increased across the board, or shifted from one mission to another, or transferred to other agencies altogether?

THE OPTIONS

Here are some crucial warnings to keep in mind as you read the distilled discussion of the options below and the draft speeches that follow:

- The speech you would actually give to Congress or similarly involved audiences would be more general than the drafts provided here. It would also likely blend various elements from several of the following speeches. The secretary of defense would be responsible for providing greater rationale and detail to support your choices.

- None of these defense policy choices represents a fundamental shift in U.S. foreign policy. Each assumes that the United States will stay firmly engaged in global security affairs, continue to lead in its military alliances, and keep American forces abroad on both temporary and long-term deployments. Options representing a major foreign policy shift were not considered. Thus, none of the choices presented here would transform the United States into a global policeman, capable of unilaterally exercising what has sometimes been called "benevolent hegemony." Nor does any choice require reductions of a magnitude that would signify a new isolationism, called by some "strategic independence." The options outlined here span the broad middle ground of possible directions, each offering a different way of supporting the same basic foreign policy goals.

- Major changes in strategic nuclear policy, such as the large-scale cuts that you and Russian President Vladimir Putin agreed to in Moscow in May 2002, are discussed principally in the "Cooperative Defense" alternative, where they comprise part of a major reduction in traditional military forces. But as mentioned above, changes in nuclear policy could also fit into any of the four options. National missile defense (NMD), or as the Pentagon now calls it, ballistic missile defense (BMD), which became a major issue in the 2000 campaign and continues to be one of your major priorities, is treated most thoroughly in the "Revolutionary Transformation" alternative. These and other nuclear issues are being pressed by vocal groups of political leaders and defense intellectuals. One group, primarily composed of Republicans, wants a major effort to develop a robust national defense against long-range missile attacks from rogue nations. You must make a major decision in this area very soon if you expect to have even a rudimentary system in place before the 2004 election. Your decision will involve not only whether and when to deploy, but also the type of system—specifically, land-, sea-, air-, or space-based, or some combination of the four. A second group argues for a determined and gradual elimination, or virtual elimination, of nuclear weapons. We assume that although you would not want to eliminate all strategic nuclear weapons, you obviously must carry out the reduction to between 1,700 and 2,200 warheads outlined in your May 2002 agreement with President Putin.

- Finally, the alternatives do not delve into specialized, but very important, defense debates, such as improving procurement procedures and policies or reorganizing the military services (for example, creating separate services for tactical aircraft, strategic nuclear forces, space, or information warfare). As former Vice President Al Gore discovered in his reinvention of the government initiative, and as your own Office of Management and Budget review of DoD performance noted, there are a lot of potential savings involved here—and even more bureaucratic and political grief.

The summary of each option characterizes the chief challenges to our security and outlines a plan to align our forces accordingly. A brief explanation of the strengths, weakness, and political impact of each option follows.

OPTION ONE: AN ENHANCED DEFENSE

September 11, 2001, provided a wake-up call, alerting us to the new missions our military must take on and the new capabilities our armed forces must develop. But the new tasks we assign to our military will not simply replace the pre-September 11 missions. They will have to be added to the list of critical functions the U.S. armed services are already performing around the world.

We must make sure our military can protect the homeland, deter, preempt, or defeat global threats, and handle major regional contingencies in which the U.S. national interest is at stake. Experience also teaches that we need a margin against the unexpected and a force robust enough to win at relatively low cost in American blood and treasure. Not much help can be expected from broader collective security arrangements that have failed of late. Even dependable allies are growing less capable of aiding the United States in large-scale combat missions like Operation Desert Storm; or even in less demanding military operations such as the Kosovo air campaign, where American aircraft had to fly the vast majority of the missions; or in Afghanistan, where only the United States possessed the "smart" munitions necessary to rout the ground forces of the Taliban and al Qaeda.

We cannot tell the American people that we will not spend whatever is necessary to defend this great country. Current strategy and budgets threaten to leave the United States with a military that is underfunded for performing technological change, overstretched by peacekeeping and other peripheral operations, and unprepared to protect core interests from potentially larger threats. Some have even described the current defense budget situation as a coming train wreck. Unless we tailor our forces to meet major operational challenges, conduct limited peacekeeping, and fund technological advances, we face a potentially catastrophic failure of deterrence and fighting ability.

The solution is to refocus U.S. strategy on the war on terror and on the deterrence of major threats in areas of vital geographic interest. This change requires slightly increasing the size of U.S. forces; procuring new equipment, especially with an eye toward technological innovation; increasing the number and quality of our Special Forces troops; deploying a robust NMD system; not using our forces in peacekeeping; and relying more on our allies for small regional missions. To achieve all of these goals simultaneously, we need to gradually increase the share of GDP devoted to defense from 3.5 to 4 percent by 2007.

Advantages
- Provides a force robust enough to give us high confidence in our ability to deter, preempt, or defeat current and future threats—foreseen or unforeseen.

- Transforms the military from a Cold War force to one suitable for meeting the challenges of the 21st century.

- Fully funds a realistic modernization program to replace equipment stocks left over from the 1970s and 1980s.

- Solves problems such as the deterioration in readiness due to the high pace of current operations being shouldered by a much smaller force.

- Enhances the quality of life of our service personnel enough to meet recruiting and retention challenges.

Disadvantages
- Requires continued, massive increases in defense spending at a time when there are many competing claims on a federal budget that is already in deficit.

- Eliminates the U.S. role in peacekeeping and humanitarian relief operations, thereby decreasing U.S. influence in these matters.

- Makes non-traditional threats such as ethnic violence or international crime a lesser priority.

- Possibly misses the potential and comparative advantage of achieving major technological breakthroughs at lower cost, since modernization will be incremental and, as a result, could cost more in the long run.

Political Impact
- Congressional debate over this approach will likely feature support from a bipartisan coalition of post–Cold War hawks and from former secretaries of defense such as James Schlesinger and Harold Brown. This group has already pressured Congress into adding substantial sums (as much as 5 percent a year) to the defense budget during each of the past six years. President Bill Clinton added more than $200 billion to his own five-year defense program in his last two years in office; in your first year in the White House, you increased the defense budget by $80 billion. Opposition will likely come from supporters of peacekeeping missions, traditional liberals, and tax-cutting conservatives. To rebut their arguments, advocates of enhanced defense can point out that the increased spending in this option can be offset by savings from reforming Pentagon management practices and by raising defense expenditures to

their historic levels. As indicated in Figures 1 and 2, defense today consumes only 3.5 percent of our GDP and 16 percent of federal outlays, about half their shares of a decade ago.

- In the Pentagon, all the services will likely give strong support to this option, as it reaffirms traditional roles, adds to force structure and investment, and addresses the concerns of the Joint Chiefs of Staff about overextending the military and about the quality of life of the troops.

- Among the general public, support cannot be expected without vigorous presidential leadership that clearly enunciates the problems caused by current strategy, presents a realistic picture of the military's role in the war on terror, and explains the expected defense budget "train wreck" if program costs continue to far exceed planned funding.

- Among our allies, a reduction in the number of U.S. ground troops available for multinational peacekeeping-type operations will not be well received and will likely make it more difficult to achieve the desired outcome in these situations, at least until the European Defense Initiative becomes a reality.

OPTION TWO: A REVOLUTIONARY TRANSFORMATION

As you noted in the 2000 campaign and as the events of September 11 demonstrated, the U.S. military must be transformed if it is to deal with the very different kinds of challenges that are likely to emerge in this new century. The military threats to our nation in the short term will be primarily asymmetrical. Over the long term, by contrast, military powers with the strength or technological prowess to challenge our Cold War–era military will emerge as the chief threat to U.S. security. Our forces are still designed to fight the wars of the past, yet we are in the middle of a far-reaching technological revolution. We could therefore face a catastrophe one day, with potentially ineffective weapons and obsolete tactics. The spread of technology, the high cost of innovation, and the long lead time for modernization all require action now if we are to be safe later. The United States is overly prepared to meet diminishing threats (such as conventional warfare against North Korea or Iraq) and still too focused on Europe, where a large-scale war is now almost unthinkable. Meanwhile, we are in danger of wasting precious opportunities: to stay ahead of future competitors (such as China), to deal with asymmetrical threats (such as terrorism and information warfare), and to defend our own territory from ballistic missile threats from rogue states. We have already seen the tragic results of such myopia: on September 11, 2001, this country paid a heavy price for ignoring the asymmetrical threat of terrorism.

The United States must act now in two ways: by taking full advantage of the "revolution in military affairs" and by shifting the military's primary focus to Asia. An agile, innovative, and high-tech U.S. military force will be dramatically more effective if it uses a space-, sea-, air-, and ground-based network of sensors to pinpoint enemy forces, and a similar network of precision-guided munitions to destroy them from long range. Exploiting new technologies and fielding a very different information-age force will not require a major increase in spending, but it will necessitate major changes in spending priorities and drastic revisions in U.S. doctrine, strategy, and force structure. To accomplish such objectives, the United States will have to accept the limited risk that its forces will not be able to handle all current contingencies, such as the peacekeeping missions in the Balkans or the one in the Sinai Peninsula. We will have to call upon allies, particularly in Europe, the United Nations, and other collective security groups to do more, especially in costly peacekeeping interventions. These risks, however, are more than offset by the edge that such a strategy will give the United States well into the future. Innovation should be restored to its traditional role as America's most decisive strength. Spending priorities within the defense budget will be readjusted, but there will be no major budget increases beyond those made in the last three years.

Advantages
- Harnesses traditional American competence in technology and innovation to ensure U.S. primacy against any conceivable military threat for 50 years or more.

- Protects more effectively against new threats such as terrorism, information warfare, WMD, and ballistic missiles.

- Solves the dilemma of a slow modernization that could cost more and produce less if carried out over the long run, and is affordable at current spending levels if savings in Pentagon management and financial practices are achieved.

- Takes into account the end of the Cold War and the reduced threat of major war in Europe, as well as the growing importance of the Asian theater to U.S. security.

Disadvantages
- Reduces the U.S. role in many current peacekeeping operations, and thus accepts the risk of such conflicts spreading out of control.

- Generates considerable institutional instability in each of the services and the Pentagon, as old bureaucratic and organizational structures are challenged and supplanted by new ones.

- Produces a force that might be too specialized to be helpful in the event of labor-intensive threats, such as low-intensity conflicts and peacekeeping and humanitarian relief operations.

- Increases U.S. reliance on European allies in the near term for undertaking some global security tasks, such as regional peacekeeping and humanitarian operations.

Political Impact
- In Congress, this approach is likely to be supported by only a small but influential group of defense analysts willing to take risks on national defense. Strong opposition will arise among members from those districts where the legacy systems are built.

Presidential leadership—to emphasize the low level of current risk and huge future benefits—will be critical.

- In the Pentagon, the approach is likely to be supported most vigorously by the Air Force (because of the emphasis on outer space) and fairly well supported by the Marine Corps. Resistance, largely to the pace of these changes, will come from elements in the Navy (particularly the naval aviation community) and the Army.

- This approach will garner support from business and some parts of the defense industry, since much of the new military technology will be borrowed "off-the-shelf" from civilian high-technology firms. But there will be resistance from those elements of the defense industry that produce the legacy systems.

- Among the general public, you can expect support if you use the bully pulpit to provide inspiration, as was done with the space program of the 1960s. And like the space program, public support will falter as expensive experiments and systems fail, which is inevitable.

- This new approach will aggravate the growing incompatibility between U.S. and allied forces. As was evident during the Kosovo air war in the spring of 1999 and in the campaign against the Taliban, even our European allies are falling steadily further behind the United States in adapting new technologies to the military and would be disconcerted by additional U.S. technical advances.

OPTION THREE: AN EVOLUTIONARY TRANSFORMATION

Regardless of how much the United States spends on defense, it cannot buy perfect security. As shown in Figure 3, even if one accounts for inflation, President Clinton's last defense budget was higher than each of the final defense budgets of Presidents Eisenhower, Nixon, and Ford, and it totaled more than 90 percent of the average Cold War defense budget. The additions you have made since taking office have now brought defense spending to 15 percent above average Cold War levels.

Some military leaders claim that current budget levels cannot support the modified two-war strategy outlined in the 2001 QDR. Yet to make this assertion, they assume that the strategy must be executable at extremely low levels of risk. Their pessimism also relies on a severe overestimation of the capabilities of potential adversaries such as Iraq and North Korea and a severe underestimation of the capabilities of our own armed forces, which performed so well in Afghanistan. In fact, the Iraqi and North Korean military capabilities have declined markedly, both in absolute terms and relative to U.S. forces, since the Bottom-Up Review of 1993. Similarly, the claim by some that peacekeeping operations are stretching the Pentagon too thin is also an exaggeration. The military has less than 10,000 people deployed in these peacekeeping operations. A greater percentage of the force is stationed in the United States now than on average during the Cold War.

The Pentagon does indeed have some personnel and equipment problems, but they will be solved with better management, not more money. The military uses a compensation system left over from the Great Depression and a procurement strategy that has us in an arms race with ourselves. Paying people for performance and moving to a defined contribution plan for retirement as well as privatizing the health and housing systems will save money and be more attractive to the troops. Skipping deployment of a generation of new weapon systems will allow the services to buy more of the current generation, which are the best in the world, and to maintain our technological edge without increasing money for procurement. If the Pentagon enacts these changes to its compensation system and adjusts its procurement strategy by skipping the deployment of a generation of new systems, it will be more than capable of carrying out the modified two-MRC strategy while still making important contributions to peacekeeping operations—that is, doing everything from providing combat troops as in Kosovo and Bosnia, to simply helping with intelligence and logistics as we did in East Timor—and playing a major role in the war on terror.

Advantages
- Allows us to deal with conventional military threats, the need for action in smaller contingencies such as Bosnia and Kosovo, and threats as varied as WMD proliferation, the spread of ballistic missile technology, and terrorism.

- Reforms the compensation system and procurement strategy to allow the military to cope with its recruitment and retention challenges and shortages of equipment.

- Offers steady capabilities and policy to support the current U.S. defense posture.

Disadvantages
- Does not prioritize threats or missions.

- Does not clearly prepare for future threats that are markedly different from current challenges, potentially leaving the United States vulnerable to a "Pearl Harbor" in space or via the Internet.

- Depends on the Pentagon's ability to reform its compensation system and procurement strategy.

Political Impact
- The Pentagon and its allies on Capitol Hill will be unhappy if you do not increase defense spending and reduce peacekeeping operations. But majorities in Congress, among U.S. allies, and in the American public will be content to leave spending levels at about $400 billion. Although there will always be vocal dissenters, any major changes in defense policy and spending in a time of peace (notwithstanding the war on terrorism, peace still prevails among the major powers) will be more controversial than maintaining the status quo.

OPTION FOUR: A COOPERATIVE DEFENSE

The technological revolution in communications, transportation, and commerce that has been an integral part of globalization has its dark side, which was made all too clear on September 11, 2001. That day, we learned the hard way that the most clear and present dangers to the United States no longer come from other states and we no longer will primarily face state-to-state conflict. Instead, global problems such as WMD proliferation, terrorism, drugs, poverty, AIDS, and global warming are the greatest threats to the United States. And they are problems that cannot be solved by the actions of any one state, powerful as it may be.

Our military showed its capability to handle any potential military contingency with its stellar performance in Afghanistan. As a result, no military competitor will dare challenge the United States directly. We therefore should put our resources into the cooperative efforts that offer our only hope of dealing with the intractable international problems described above. We must also refocus our efforts on preventive diplomatic efforts and increase funding for the State Department.

We have learned that what we once perceived as smaller ethnic and civil conflicts can in fact threaten our vital national interests; now, more than ever, some military action will be called for to protect our interests and values.

As matters now stand, however, the international capacity to deal with these intrastate conflicts remains limited: either the United States leads a military intervention, or nothing happens. If we get involved, we run risks that might outstrip our interests; but if we fail to involve ourselves militarily, we risk small conflicts' burgeoning into larger ones or damaging our leadership role. This quandary puts the United States in a situation where it is not sure what kinds of forces to build—for peacekeeping-type operations, futuristic space and information warfare, or Gulf War–type combat—and leads to dangerous confusion.

Thus stymied since the Cold War, our concept of national security and military strategy is still built around outdated concepts of state-to-state conflict, massive nuclear deterrence, and large conventional forces. Conflicts such as the ones in Bosnia and Afghanistan, as well as new economic, developmental, and environmental problems, are more relevant to national security today than is Cold War thinking. The United States must tailor its forces to the conflicts of today's world. But the United States cannot do everything, and the United Nations is not at this juncture capable of playing a major role in global security. Thus, America must take the lead in building the capabilities of regional security organizations and the United Nations, as well as in creating informal networks of allies to intervene with us in the complex conflict situations that we continue to face.

At the moment, these international institutions are not prepared to accept greater responsibility. Unless the United States helps others develop the power to act, the burden will always fall on Washington. Building collective security institutions and capabilities will be a long, controversial, and difficult process. It must begin with a determined U.S. effort to forge political cohesion in old and new international organizations and to help these organizations develop the necessary military capabilities to intervene. On a parallel track, an emphasis on preventive diplomacy and multilateral responses will reduce the need for large deployments of U.S. forces.

Multilateralism and cooperation should also extend to the areas of missile defense and arms control. Building networks of mutual assurance through arms-control agreements will allow us to take the lead in greatly reducing global nuclear arsenals, including reducing our own to no more than 1,000, and stemming WMD proliferation—and to do so more effectively than would unilateral deployment of an NMD system, which we should abandon. In addition, we need to expand our nonproliferation programs and cooperative threat initiatives such as the Nunn-Lugar programs and drastically increase funding for foreign aid. In sum, this approach, a new form of collective security, would lessen the pressures on the U.S. military to do everything and thus allow us to cut defense spending by 15 to 20 percent from its current levels (now 15 percent higher than what we spent during the Cold War) and finally achieve a real peace dividend.

Advantages
- Realigns a Cold War defense policy and military force structure with current threats and security challenges.

- Reduces defense spending to levels more consistent with other demands on the federal budget, which is once again in deficit, and more in line with the levels of our allies.

- Allows the United States to shift resources to confront "new agenda" threats such as global warming, refugees, and terrorism.

- Takes full advantage of multilateral cooperation and keeps the United States involved in peacekeeping-type operations without overcommitment.

- Enhances the prospects for an arms-control regime that will reduce the number of existing nuclear weapons, prevent the spread of nuclear weapons and ballistic missile technology, and make the deployment of a $240 billion NMD system unnecessary.

Disadvantages
- Reduces the capability for rapid combat operations on the scale of Operation Desert Storm or larger.

- Sends signals of retrenchment and possible isolation to allies and adversaries by reducing U.S. deployments and forces stationed overseas, potentially creating a power vacuum that could encourage the development of a near-peer competitor.

- Increases U.S. reliance on uncertain allies and undependable international organizations for helping to protect U.S. national interests until the necessary changes can be made.

- Raises issues regarding the foreign command of U.S. troops in multilateral operations led by allies.

Political Impact
- In Congress, this approach will meet opposition on both sides of the aisle from advocates of strong U.S. military power who vehemently oppose greater reliance on the United Nations and other multilateral organizations, as well as military operations not led or dominated by the United States. On the other

hand, supporters of humanitarian interventions will endorse this approach.

- Some of these same advocates of a strong U.S. military will clamor for deploying NMD as soon as possible. Arms-control advocates will oppose it.

- In the Pentagon, all services will openly oppose the downgrading of U.S. capability.

- Many constituencies will resist reductions in our nuclear forces to 1,000 warheads, although there is new support among former military and some political leaders for movement on this issue.

- Most U.S. allies will welcome the multilateral spirit of this policy, although a few will denounce the move as a U.S. retreat from responsibility.

RECOMMENDATION

Convene your senior national security team informally to review this memo. If the sense emerges that present defense policy will put the United States at significant future risks, direct the secretary of defense to prepare a new draft speech—with any supporting studies—presenting the new approach.

Table 1. U.S. Defense Policy Reviews

	Actual Force 1991	Bush Base Force Review 1991	Bottom-Up Review 1993	Quadrennial Defense Review 1997	Quadrennial Defense Review 2001
Army (Divisions)	19 Active* 16 Reserve**	14 Active* 8 Reserve**	11 Active* 5+ Reserve**	11 Active* 5 Reserve**	10 Active* 8 Reserve**
Navy	528 Ships 15 Carriers***	450 Ships 13 Carriers***	346 Ships 12 Carriers***	300+ Ships 12 Carriers***	300+ Ships 12 Carriers***
Marine Corps (Personnel)	194,000 Active 45,000 Reserve	159,000 Active 35,000 Reserve	174,000 Active 42,000 Reserve	172,000 Active 37,800 Reserve	173,000 Active 40,000 Reserve
Total Uniformed Personnel	2,130,000 Active 1,170,000 Reserve	1,640,000 Active 920,000 Reserve	1,450,000 Active 900,000 Reserve	1,360,000 Active 835,000 Reserve	1,450,000 Active 864,000 Reserve

*Accounts for separate brigades and regiments not organized into divisions.

**Accounts for separate brigades not organized into divisions but does not include two cadre divisions.

***Includes training carrier.

Table 2. International Comparison of Defense Spending
(In millions of 1999 constant dollars)

	Defense Spending		Per Capita		Percent of GDP	
	1998	1999	1998	1999	1998	1999
United States	279,702	283,096	1,034	1,036	3.1	3.1
Argentina	5,365	5,418	149	148	1.8	1.9
Brazil	18,781	15,978	116	98	3.2	2.7
Canada	7,677	7,504	265	257	1.2	1.2
Chile	3,071	2,694	208	181	3.8	4.0
China	38,191	39,889	31	32	5.3	5.4
Colombia	2,574	2,164	63	52	3.2	2.8
Cuba	765	750	68	67	5.3	4.8
Egypt	2,888	2,988	47	48	3.4	3.4
France	40,834	37,893	693	640	2.8	2.7
Germany	33,802	31,117	412	379	1.5	1.6
India	13,594	14,991	14	15	3.2	3.4
Iran	5,879	5,711	95	91	6.5	6.2
Iraq	1,428	1,500	66	68	7.3	7.6
Israel	9,339	8,846	1,560	1,465	9.3	8.9
Japan	38,482	40,383	305	319	1.0	0.9
Korea, North	2,086	2,100	97	98	14.3	14.3
Korea, South	10,461	12,088	225	257	2.4	3.0
Kuwait	3,674	3,275	1,670	1,440	14.3	11.1
Malaysia	1,891	3,158	88	146	2.6	4.0
Mexico	3,907	4,289	39	42	0.9	0.9
Pakistan	4,078	3,523	29	24	6.6	5.7
Philippines	1,521	1,627	21	22	2.3	2.1
Russia	57,107	56,800	390	380	5.3	5.1
Saudi Arabia	21,303	21,876	1,081	1,099	16.2	15.5
Singapore	4,936	4,696	1,275	1,174	5.6	5.6
South Africa	1,900	1,755	49	44	1.4	1.3
Taiwan	14,447	14,964	668	687	4.8	5.2
Turkey	8,955	10,183	143	156	4.2	5.5
United Kingdom	38,093	36,876	650	628	2.7	2.6

SOURCE: International Institute for Strategic Studies, *The Military Balance*, 2000/2001.

SPEECH ONE: AN ENHANCED DEFENSE

A plan to reduce the strain on small and underfunded U.S. military forces by increasing force size; adding substantially to the defense budget; decreasing U.S. participation in some peacekeeping operations; refocusing U.S. strategy on winning the war against global terrorism, deterrence of the "axis of evil" states, and war fighting; and investing in the technologies of the future, including a robust NMD. Cumulatively, these measures move toward correcting the imbalance between our current strategy and force structure.

Members of Congress and My Fellow Americans:

Thank you for welcoming me to Capitol Hill this evening. I have decided to speak directly to this special joint session of Congress because the president's first responsibility, under the Constitution, is our national defense. As the tragic events of September 11 demonstrated, we need to make difficult decisions, and we need to act soon.

The terrorist attacks have given the United States a unique opportunity to win the peace and to help construct an international order that favors democracy and prosperity. But to achieve these objectives, we must be able not only to deter aggression by terrorists with global reach and support from evil regimes, but also to deal with a range of other challenges in a highly uncertain world. It is this world, and how we must protect our country in it, that I will describe tonight.

Until now, we have attempted to meet security challenges with a military force reduced by one-third from its Cold War size. Simultaneously, we have used our troops with increasing frequency in vague, aimless peacekeeping operations and other missions short of war. As a result of this policy, we are wasting too much effort on peripheral issues. We have been shortchanging the future, spending too much on today's wrongheaded priorities and too little on tomorrow's necessities. Our defense strategy has lost its focus, and our troops are in danger of losing their essential war-fighting skills.

The plan I am proposing tonight—an enhanced defense—will set America on the right course once more and will fulfill my campaign promise to the troops that help was on the way. We will ensure that our military has the ability to protect the U.S. homeland and its forces overseas; to project and sustain power in distant theaters; to deny enemies sanctuary where they can hide and function; to protect U.S. information networks from attack; to use information technology to connect U.S. forces into a joint fighting network; and finally, to maintain unhindered access to space and protect U.S. space capabilities from enemy attack.

To do this, we must win the global war on terrorism; we must restore military capabilities by making investments in procurement, people, and modernization; and we must prepare for the future by transforming for the 21st century.

At the same time, we will raise substantially the pay and benefits of our military personnel. It is a national disgrace to have more than 1,000 of our brave soldiers, sailors, airmen, and marines on food stamps.

We will also give our military forces the resources they need, despite the substantial extra cost. September 11 has taught us once again that when it comes to America's defense, we must spend what is necessary to protect our freedom, our security, and our prosperity—not just for this generation, but to preserve peace and security for our children and our grandchildren.

In addition, we must develop and deploy a defense against intercontinental ballistic missiles. Unless the United States is protected from a missile attack by a rogue nation, such as North Korea or Iraq, or a terrorist group that obtains a weapon of mass destruction, our ability to take action around the world will suffer.

Our defense planning begins with the definition of our interests and how our military forces can best secure them. The twentieth century taught Americans that what we value most—our democratic freedoms—can be put at risk by aggression far from our shores. That century also showed us that prosperity and security are the necessary escorts of our democratic freedom. Yet just as democracy is vulnerable in this era of globalization, so too are its escorts. Our well-being here at home depends on the vital trading relationships we have forged with Europe, Asia, the Middle East, and our neighbors in the Americas. The world's economic progress relies on a broad framework of security, of which America's military forces are a vital component. U.S. troops do more than deter aggression; they also embody America's determination to work for a better world.

As a nation, we have made enormous sacrifices in lives and treasure throughout our history to preserve our democracy—indeed, to give democracy a fighting chance in the rest of the world. And in this we have succeeded. After two world wars, a third called the Cold War, and the war against al Qaeda and the Taliban in Afghanistan, our democracy is today secure and prosperous.

However, as the events of September 11 showed, it would be most unwise for Americans to take this security for granted. Terrorists with global reach and potential access to weapons of mass destruction can inflict massive damage on our homeland. And these are not the only sources of danger in the world. Let me cite just a few other examples.

In Europe, the threats of the Cold War have given way to pervasive uncertainty. Russia is still going through wrenching political and economic change a decade after communism's collapse. We have expanded NATO, while the European Union has begun the process of accommodating new members. These are large investments in the future security and prosperity of Europe that also call for a constructive U.S. relationship with Russia, and such has been our objective. Even though President Vladimir Putin and I are currently working well together, we must be realistic about his regime. No one can forecast Russia's future course, and in the past we have often been surprised as Moscow veered sharply between reform and revolution, cooperation and conflict.

A similar caution should govern our policy in Asia, where China is undergoing a transformation. We hope that the current authoritarian government will give way in time to real democracy, but my responsibility as president is to do more than hope. There are American interests that need to be safeguarded, especially the freedom of shipping lanes and international airspace and the restriction of Chinese weapons exports to unfriendly nations. In 1996, President Clinton had to send two aircraft carrier battle groups to the Taiwan Strait when China threatened to disrupt Taiwanese elections. As that episode showed, even in times of peace, a robust and well-trained American military provides a healthy deterrent against those who would seek to disrupt the peace. Good intentions and vigorous diplomacy will not always be enough in dealing with other great powers whose interests may at times conflict with ours. As you know from that unfortunate incident in the spring of 2001, the Navy and Air Force must fly surveillance flights off the coast of China to monitor China's continuing military buildup.

Then there are the states that constitute the axis of evil. American troops today face a North Korean regime that has put its people on the brink of starvation and remains without allies. And despite its overtures to South Korea, this same government remains armed to the teeth, has its troops poised to invade South Korea, and has tested a long-range missile capable of hitting the United States with a weapon of mass destruction attached. In the Middle East, Iraq still possesses enough military power to threaten its neighbors in the absence of U.S. air, sea, and land power. Iran, a supporter of terrorism, seeks nuclear and other weapons of mass destruction. Both states are located in the Persian Gulf, which has resources vital to U.S. and allied security. And, as we have seen in the continuing confrontation with Iraq, deterring these states still requires that the United States have large and readily deployable forces whose primary duty is to go to war if necessary. No one should doubt that both Tehran and Baghdad would commit aggression if U.S. forces were not deployed in the Gulf and poised to stop them.

Yet another danger is the spread of ballistic missile technology and weapons of mass destruction—nuclear, chemical, or biological—that might fall into the hands of terrorists or states that sponsor terrorism and possibly be used against the United States itself. Nor can we ignore the savage civil wars, such as those that occurred in Bosnia, Kosovo, and Macedonia, that threaten to spill over borders, spreading chaos and desperation in their wake.

The uncertainties and perils of these many challenges mean that we need a large and well-trained military prepared to deal with a broad range of contingencies, perhaps even simultaneously in more than one region. The world has changed profoundly since the end of the Cold War. Thus, the capacity to respond to the new threats posed by terrorism, ethnic violence, international crime, and failing states must now be a part of our national security strategy. But the extent to which these new threats should constitute the focus of our strategy has very much been oversold. Like many other turning points in history, the end of the Cold War was trumpeted by many observers as the dawn of the era of globalization and therefore the end of conflict between the world's major powers, all of which were now market-oriented, economically interdependent, and democratically leaning states. We were told that the military challenges of the post–Cold War world would not be akin to deterring the Soviet Union or even deterring Iraq and North Korea. The new military threats would be like those we encountered in Somalia, Haiti, and Bosnia.

I must tell you, however, that I believe that the new missions of our time are not so new and not so critical that they should make the world's only superpower lose sight of its most crucial security tasks. These are the tasks that only the United States can perform, the traditional missions that keep the major powers free from conflict and the major systems of the world functioning in good order.

Our priorities should be clear. Think of it this way: If worse came to worst and we failed to deal with international terrorists, a renewed Russian threat, an emerging Chinese challenge, or Iraqi or Iranian aggression in the Persian Gulf, the very foundations of our security and prosperity would be shaken. If we deter trouble in these areas, however, we can also deal with other issues such as failed states, the spread of AIDS, and world poverty. If we cannot, a lot of other issues will not matter. That is why in Europe and in Asia, for example, U.S. forces are working with our allies in NATO and Japan to encourage Russia and China to join an international community they once opposed. Our forces there are like firefighters. Just because the fire has gone out, that is no reason to disband the fire department. The peace dividend should not be viewed as a chance to do away with a military that effectively deters threats to global security. The peace dividend is continued peace— and we must continue to work hard for it.

A robust and well-trained American military force provides insurance against a major power threat, but it must also be capable of deterring or, if need be, preempting threats from evil states or terrorists with a global reach, and supporting U.S. diplomacy in the world's trouble spots. To do all this, our troops must be trained to act in case deterrence fails—in other words, to fight and to win wars as they have done in Afghanistan. The American way of war gives every advantage to our troops by emphasizing the need to achieve a rapid and overwhelming victory. This will not always be achieved with the relative ease of Operation Desert Storm or the air campaign in Kosovo or the war against the Taliban, but it should always be our goal. There is nothing heroic in deploying just enough American forces to produce a stalemate or a slugfest on the battlefield. As commander in chief, I can assure you that I will field fighting forces that are well-trained and large enough to win a quick and decisive victory in any future conflict.

At the end of the Cold War, the United States fielded a superb military, ranging from a broad-based nuclear arsenal to large, highly trained conventional air, sea, and ground forces with global reach, all backed by an advanced defense industry and capable reserves. Expecting more peaceful times, we reduced our active forces by more than one-third. But things have not worked out as expected. We have actually sent our soldiers, sailors, marines, and airmen on missions abroad more often than during the Cold War—more than 40 times in the Clinton administration, compared with 14 times under my father's administration and 16 times under President Ronald Reagan's administration. Some missions have been short, focused, and effective humanitarian operations. Others, such as the intervention in Somalia, began that way but turned into something else. In that country, as in Bosnia and Kosovo and now Macedonia, our troops have been used to keep the peace and to build nations. Some of these operations, such as Bosnia and

Kosovo, have required a much more prolonged and expensive effort than we first anticipated.

Our desire to help carries a cost. All the emphasis on the here and now, on these complex operations that are neither war nor peace, has undercut our ability to protect our homeland and deter major conflicts.

Loss of Focus

First, our military is losing its focus on war-fighting skills, the most essential capabilities of American defense. Peacekeeping operations put our troops into situations more akin to police work than to soldiering. Seizing ground, taking the offensive, and defeating the enemy are out. Restraint, forbearance, caution, and diplomacy are in. Large numbers of our troops and officers are therefore gaining much experience in peacekeeping at the expense of their skill in war fighting.

Being prepared to conduct warfare effectively on the scale of Operation Desert Storm requires maintaining a sense of urgency and focus at every level in our military training. We would like to think that peacekeepers are equally trained for fighting wars, but this is simply not true.

Extensive retraining is required to bring our troops on peace-keeping duty back to combat readiness. I would like to say that the results have been worth the risks, but I cannot. We have all learned a lesson in how difficult it is to repair societies torn apart by civil war or to revive a sense of nationhood in peoples who have lost it. In the last decade, we have refocused too large a part of our military effort on humanitarian missions, the outcomes of which are temporary, fragile, or easily reversed, as in Haiti.

Hollowing Out the Force

Second, using smaller forces more often has taken our troops to the edge of endurance and beyond. That threatens a slow hollowing out of our military. Let me explain what I mean by "hollow out." The key to our military capability is the quality of our troops. Today Americans volunteer to defend our country; there is no draft, and I do not propose to reinstate one. But just consider what has happened to our volunteer army since 1989. The number of active-duty soldiers has decreased by 36 percent. In spite of the defense budget's increases in the last two years, spending is still down by 10 percent compared to a decade ago, even before the deployments to Central Asia. Meanwhile, the number of missions has increased by 300 percent. What does all this do to our troops and their families? Listen to what they are saying. An officer at a major base used these words, and I quote:

> The more you take down the force, while keeping the same level of operations, the harder the remaining force works, which means more people get out, which means the remainder works harder, which means more of them get out, and now you're in this death spiral, right into the ground.

Those are alarming words, but even more alarming are those of a veteran colonel: "What broke the army in Vietnam was the stress on the noncommissioned officers. ... The families said, 'Enough of this,' and they all got out."

Shortages of middle-grade and noncommissioned officers persist in all the services. In the 1990s, the Air Force and the Navy lost experienced pilots at an unprecedented rate and are now short several hundred. Extended overseas duty is taking its toll on our Navy, putting great pressure on family life. And because too many units are undermanned during their training cycles people do not train together at full strength and they do not gain the experience they need to work as a team. Less training and less effective training also increases the risk of tragic accidents. The overall result is creeping hollowness and poor morale. It happened before, 30 years ago. We must not let it happen again.

Obsolescence
Third, we have begun to risk the future quality of our forces. We expected to live off the large equipment stocks left over from the Cold War for a long time. But unanticipated uses of the military abroad, obsolete equipment, and reduced budgets have taken their toll. The defense industry itself has downsized in lock step with our overall defense reductions. Meanwhile, we have had to finance operations out of the maintenance funds, and the maintenance funds out of the procurement budget, essentially trapping

the military in a vicious cycle. And, as I noted earlier, the defense budget itself has dropped by 10 percent. Not since before Pearl Harbor have we had a defense budget that took a smaller share of GDP or a lower percentage of federal government expenditures than the current one.

Something had to give. And something did.

We can fix our readiness and maintenance problems fairly quickly, but the problem of inadequate procurement of new equipment has no quick fix. Procurement takes time, lots of time. With 40 percent less money than 1998 to buy new and replacement equipment, we have stopped buying tanks and other weapons systems that have proven themselves in battle. We cannot afford nearly the number of ships that we have plans to use in the future. Within the current budget, we will not be able to acquire about 40 percent of planned aircraft. By the year 2010, almost all of our tanks and planes will be older than the soldiers or airmen driving and flying them. In short, our modernization plans have been severely curtailed.

It is a bad time for us to be in such a predicament. In our everyday lives, the extraordinary technological changes of our era affect virtually everything we do. A military revolution is also under way that we cannot afford to miss. This revolution promises a more effective defense, ranging from new antimissile systems to more precise detection of an enemy's location and rapid, surefire reaction.

Such military revolutions have happened before, and you can ask the veterans of the war in Afghanistan, for example, to compare their experience with that of their fathers in Vietnam or their grandfathers in World War II. We must investigate this revolution and invest in the military hardware, software, and skills to use it. Today, we are not doing enough of that.

I want to assure you that, as we have seen in Afghanistan since October 2001, over the short term there is no danger that we will be inferior to those who might challenge us. We still retain the edge given us by the investments of a previous generation. But I also want to tell you that we must look beyond today and even tomorrow. We cannot risk a trend that could leave us with an obsolete, under-equipped force. We must make new investments now—but in a sensible way. We will not sacrifice the capabilities of our current force in a mad dash to invest heavily in yet-to-be proven technologies. Instead, we will launch a concerted effort to modernize our forces while maintaining a large and well-prepared military for near-term threats.

The time has clearly come for us to change our ways. I am therefore asking for your support for a three-point plan, a truly enhanced defense policy. This plan will:

- Restore the proper focus of our forces on deterrence and war fighting;

- Make investments to meet the threats of the future; and

- Give our military the numbers and resources it needs to do the job efficiently.

1. Restore the Proper Focus.

Our overall military objective remains the same as ever. We should do our utmost to deter or preempt attacks on the United States, its allies, or U.S. interests. But if war comes, then we must win with as few casualties as possible. Those who defend us must therefore be trained to fight and win wars as their first duty. Ultimately, that capability is our best assurance of keeping the peace.

A force with this war-fighting capability will be able to meet the potential challenges to our security and, above all, to win the global war on terrorism and prevent aggression or the threat of aggression in Europe, Asia, and the Middle East. These are the areas where we are deployed forward, where our interests are vital. As I noted earlier, a failure to protect these interests would shake the very foundations of our security and prosperity. However unlikely it may seem at the moment, we must also be prepared to deal with a new Russian problem; a turn for the worse in China; or aggression, perhaps simultaneously, by Iran, North Korea, or Iraq, which in the last case may bring about a regime change in Baghdad.

You may have heard of the current Pentagon strategy, which focuses on the need for our forces to swiftly defeat two aggressors at the same time, while preserving the option for one major offensive to occupy an aggressor's capital and replace the regime. I do not believe that this strategy should be the alpha and the omega of American military efforts around the globe, but it does highlight an important capability to have. However, given the smaller size of today's military, our involvement in the war on terrorism and in peacekeeping operations, and a smaller defense budget, I am not convinced that we actually could wage war against two aggressors simultaneously if the need arose. The plan I propose tonight will restore to the military the tools for this capability and do so with a strategy that is refocused on deterrence and combat readiness. Such a strategy will allow America not only to respond effectively to the most serious threats but to deter them from arising in the first place.

A proper focus on the gravest potential threats also allows us to evaluate other, lesser problems. This is the place to say a word about peacekeeping and military interventions short of war, activities that have increasingly preoccupied our forces over the past decade.

There will be times when we must use force short of war to protect our interests. When we do intervene, however, common sense will be our guide. That means not risking the lives of our men and women on vague and aimless deployments. We will not intervene unless we are certain that it truly serves our interests and that by doing so, we are not reducing our ability to undertake other, more important military operations. Common sense also tells us that each operation should have a clearly defined goal, decisive means of accomplishing the goal, and a gauge of success or failure.

Furthermore, we must be realistic about what we can and cannot achieve. No one should expect American military intervention to heal the rift between families in a civil war or to rebuild a nation unwilling to rebuild itself.

Ultimately, we must protect our own interests. Fortunately, these interests are shared by many other nations. Although the majority of our allies have cut defense spending by an even greater margin than we have, they still make important contributions to deterrence. They also lend crucial assistance in peacekeeping operations, as we have seen in the Balkans and now in Afghanistan. Although the United States is the only power capable of projecting and sustaining significant combat power, friendly nations play an increasingly important role. There is neither a reason nor a need for the United States to supply the bulk of the ground forces, for example, in every such operation. Many of our allies, especially in Europe, have turned the focus of their militaries away from fighting wars and toward peacekeeping. Our NATO partners are in the process of establishing a European defense force for this exact purpose. We should take advantage of these differing capabilities, as we successfully did in East Timor in 1999 and in post-Taliban Afghanistan, by encouraging allies to take the lead in these peacekeeping and nation-building exercises.

Experience teaches that there is no substitute for carefully coordinated collective efforts in the pursuit of common interests.

I am confident that under these circumstances, Congress and the American people will be fully supportive of such operations. That support, in and of itself, is also a key condition for success. We know that. So do those who oppose us.

This is the time, too, to say a word about the United Nations. The United States has long been a supporter and advocate of the United Nations and its collective security responsibility. Here, too, we have had much recent experience. We can and should expect the United Nations to act as a forum for the discussion of security problems faced by the international community, as it did in helping establish the interim government in Afghanistan. But we cannot and should not expect the United Nations to substitute for unilateral action by this nation or regional alliances such as NATO in the management of military intervention.

2. Invest in the Future.

The current military procurement budget should be increased to at least $100 billion immediately to allow us to obtain the weapons we need tomorrow and develop the weapons we will need the day after tomorrow. These aims call for more hardware purchases and greater investment in research and development. We must also pay special attention to what some have called the revolution in military affairs, which encompasses both new technologies and new concepts of how to use them.

These advances promise to give us swift and precise identification of an enemy's location and more accurate weapons to defeat him—indeed, this promise already came true in Afghanistan. Smaller American forces, equipped with these new technologies, may be able to wield as much firepower as do the current, much larger formations. As we experiment with these innovations, our current organizations, doctrine, and indeed military culture may be sharply challenged. As the secretary of defense has noted, transformation is about an awful lot more than bombs and bullets and dollars and cents; it's about new approaches, it's about culture, it's about mindset and ways of thinking of things. We should have the courage and the resources to face up to these challenges even as we recognize that no "magic bullet" will solve every defense problem. And of this we can be certain: The United States is not the only country seeking to use technological change in the pursuit of military advantage.

I also want to say a word here about missile defense. The United States is very close to being able to field a ballistic missile defense system that will offer protection against a small-scale attack by an outlaw state such as North Korea at a cost we can afford. Our growing proficiency at finding and striking targets has led us closer to our objective of creating such a system. We will continue to work diligently on the Navy's upper- and lower-tier programs, the Air Force's airborne or space-based laser systems, and the Army's theater missile defense experiments and ground-based interceptors. Sometime in the near future, we will be able to build on small successes with these programs for effective regional, then national, missile defense systems that will be capable of destroying these missiles either in their boost phase or in mid-course outside the earth's atmosphere and upon reentry. Having given the proper notice, we withdrew from the Anti-Ballistic Missile Treaty in June 2002. Thus, we can now test and deploy a missile defense system without artificial constraints. Funding in this area will be increased as necessary to ensure that we can have a system in place no later than the middle of the decade.

3. Expand Both the Forces and Their Resources.

U.S. defense forces are clearly too small and underfunded for what they need to do. If the United States had to fight a conflict on the scale of the Persian Gulf War today, more than 85 percent of the active Army, the entire Marine Corps, and at least 66 percent of Air Force fighter aircraft and Navy carrier battle groups would be engaged, according to current projections. Little would be left for other emergencies, such as combating terrorists. A military must plan and prepare for more than just the reasonable and the expected—prudence would dictate that we also be well prepared for setbacks and unexpected challenges.

And by doing so, we can, in fact, prevent these surprises from happening in the first place. As we saw on September 11, for a country with global interests such as ours, it is simply too dangerous to have a small force based on the assumption that world events will unfold only as we expect them to.

I am therefore proposing an enlargement of authorized personnel from the currently planned 1.45 million to 1.6 million over the next year. Of these additional forces, a full 100,000 will be in the combat units, increasing that total by some 20 percent. This increase will give us the margin we need to ease the strain of current operations and to make more credible our commitments around the world.

I want to describe for you the main changes that an enhanced defense will make in our defense posture:

- Make additional, large increases in the pay of all our troops and close the gap between military and private-sector pay. The military will thus remain competitive with the private sector and ensure that none of the men and women in the service remains on food stamps.

- Increase substantially Pentagon budget funding for homeland security.

- Strengthen and enlarge our ground combat forces, either forward deployed or more capable of rapid deployment to our main areas of interest in Europe, Asia, and the Middle East.

- Retain Navy and Marine forces at current levels while emphasizing joint operations with ground forces where useful.

- Be more selective in the use of U.S. troops for peacekeeping missions and more insistent on an international division of labor that speaks to the unique capabilities of those nations participating in such missions.

- Redirect the efforts of the National Guard toward homeland defense and more combat service support rather than active combat duty around the globe.

- Spend more on both procurement and research and development, especially for those technologies that give us greater precision and control on the battlefield.

- Increase spending dramatically on ballistic missile defense (which includes both theater and national defense) and space defense.

- Finally, reduce our nuclear arsenal to between 1,700 and 2,200 warheads, as I agreed with President Putin in May 2002.

To carry out the proposals outlined here tonight, we will eventually need to increase defense spending to about $500 billion per year. I know some will say that we cannot afford to spend more on defense or that we should not spend more. The facts, however, tell us otherwise.

The current U.S. spending of about 3.5 percent of GDP on defense adds up to approximately 16 percent of the federal budget. This is the smallest proportion of our national wealth and the federal budget spent on defense since before Pearl Harbor. I propose to increase that proportion slightly, to 4 percent of GDP and 20 percent of future federal budgets.

The issue is not whether we can afford to spend more but rather whether we can risk spending less. Consider the figure cited by the New York City Comptroller's office, which estimates that the economic cost of the September 11 attacks to New York City alone will add up to about $100 billion over the next three years. Estimates of the cost to the national economy range from about $170 billion to nearly $250 billion a year in lost productivity, sales, jobs, airline revenue, and countless other areas. The cost in human lives, and the pain and suffering of so many thousands of Americans who lost loved ones that day, are of course incalculable. It is reckless to press our luck or gamble with our children's future by spending less than 4 percent of our GDP on defense.

The taxpayers of this nation, however, will never be satisfied with a plan that just adds resources. We know that defense can be run more efficiently. It is therefore essential that increased spending be accompanied by increased savings. My plan calculates that another $25 billion per year can be saved if we pursue:

- Further base closings;

- Privatization of military maintenance and support;

- More outsourcing of administrative and logistical tasks to private firms; and

- Reductions in management layers, especially in the Pentagon and other headquarters.

The time is also ripe for us to begin some other important changes. The Navy will build new kinds of ships, such as the Arsenal and Streetfighter, that fully exploit revolutionary technologies while also upgrading current weapons and ships. The Air Force will purchase increasing numbers of unmanned aircraft that have performed so well in Afghanistan to operate over the battlefield as well as in space while continuing to modernize its fighter aircraft. By 2010, about one-third of our aircraft will be unmanned. The Army will accelerate its efforts to reorganize into more mobile and agile units. Our reserve forces will be assigned the primary mission of homeland defense or emergency preparedness against terrorist attacks in the United States.

THE DECISION BEFORE US

My fellow Americans, I want to sum up the essence of the decision before us. The events of September 11 demonstrated to us the spectrum of troubles we must deal with today and the uncertainties we face when we look to tomorrow.

To protect our security, we must field a military force that can handle the major potential threats. It must also be capable of allowing us, in cooperation with our allies, to take on the occasional peacekeeping mission.

As the war in Afghanistan showed, we can still do all that today. But will we be able to tomorrow? I have made the case tonight that our forces have been looking too much at peacekeeping and not enough at fighting wars; that we are spending too large a percentage of our budget on current operations and not enough on the future; that our troops have lost their focus and are losing their edge; and that they are not being adequately compensated for their work. I have also argued that these problems can be remedied if we take prudent steps to focus on the major potential threats, such as terrorism and evil states; if we do less peacekeeping, and when we do it, share the burden more with our allies; if we redirect spending toward procurement and innovation; if we increase the pay and size of our forces; and if we raise the defense budget by 0.5 percent of GDP, while boldly cutting costs. It may seem strange on the surface to offer a force that does less with more—but in order to correct our priorities, properly fund our forces, reduce the crippling strain on our troops, and invest in the future, it must be done.

Perhaps we should think of it this way. Our defense is an insurance policy. To keep that protection for the future, we need a little more insurance now, even at the cost of a slightly higher premium. As president, I can propose a plan, but without the support of you in Congress and the American people, nothing will happen. Matters will drift until events—sometimes tragic events—dictate a change. We do not want to risk the hard-won gains of the past by failing to prepare for the future. Yet this is the very risk we will run if our forces are unable to handle a major threat from international terrorists. What is truly at stake in any defense policy is the legacy we leave for the next generation of Americans. We have the opportunity today to give our children and grandchildren a world safer than the one given us by our parents and grandparents. That is the most precious legacy we can leave for posterity. That is why we need an enhanced defense.

SPEECH TWO: A REVOLUTIONARY TRANSFORMATION

A plan to take advantage of America's current overwhelming military superiority vis-à-vis its potential adversaries to radically change the U.S. military by capitalizing on revolutionary technological advances, particularly in the area of ballistic missile defense, and thereby be better prepared for the conflicts of the future within current budgetary levels.

Members of Congress and My Fellow Americans:

I have decided to speak to you this evening because we have important decisions to make about our national defense. These decisions may very well affect the security of our nation for decades to come, determining whether our generation as well as our children and grandchildren can live in peace and safety.

As far as our security goes, we live now in a time when U.S. military power is far superior to that of any other nation. The end of the Cold War has ushered in an unprecedented era of peace and cooperation among the major powers of the world. Market-based economic systems are the norm in most places around the globe, and democracy is flourishing in more countries than ever before. China has joined the World Trade Organization, Russia has been choosing new presidents through the ballot box for a decade, and relations between North and South Korea are improving. But despite this improvement in the traditional security outlook, in relations between states, we saw on September 11 a non-traditional (or asymmetrical) threat: terrorism with global reach. International terrorism affects our basic security in a different way than conflict among major powers once did.

As we did during the years between World Wars I and II, we should use this time to experiment, innovate, and prepare our military for a very different future. During those interwar decades, we experimented with aircraft carriers and naval aviation, tanks, amphibious warfare, high-speed fighter aircraft, and long-range bombers. We did all this to better prepare for future conflicts, so that they would not repeat the senseless stalemate that was the horror of World War I. Now too we must experiment with revolutionary technologies, not only to gain an advantage over our potential enemies but also to deter war more effectively. We must not waste scarce resources by keeping an overly large Cold War military force ready for action that is not likely to happen, in effect over-insuring the present at the expense of the future.

We have learned through hard experience that the secret of an effective defense is sound and timely preparation. We have also learned that in defense no less than in our domestic economy, America's success has always come from its ability to innovate, not only through scientific discoveries but also through their applications.

Military innovation is now both the challenge and the decision before us. We are in the midst of a profound revolution in military affairs. Based on the advanced technologies of the information age, this revolution is as significant to the future of warfare as were the technological advances that accompanied the industrial age in the nineteenth century. The weapons and ways of fighting wars that accompany this revolution in military affairs will change our strategy as much as the tank, the radio, the airplane, the aircraft carrier, and the long-range rocket changed the nature of warfare in the past. And the new technologies promise to give us a far more effective military than we have ever had before. Those who master this revolution will be able to meet the threats and challenges of the future. Those who do not will be condemned to obsolescence. And in warfare, obsolescence means defeat.

Fortunately, the United States today is unlikely to be challenged by a major power in Europe or Asia. We face new threats, such as terrorism and international crime, and challenges posed by evil states or ethnic conflicts. Some of these threats can be met by a broad coalition of forces that includes both our traditional allies and our former adversaries; some cannot be contained within borders. Clearly we have the opportunity—indeed, the obligation—

to redesign the U.S. military forces that were assembled more than 30 years ago to fight a war against the Soviet Union in central Europe.

We must master the technological revolution if we are to prepare the United States to deal with the challenges of the future—a high-tech future in which military innovations can spell the difference between victory and defeat. The innovations I propose will make our military not only more effective against traditional threats but better prepared for the unconventional challenges of the future. The cutting-edge military force outlined here tonight can wage a campaign like that of Operation Desert Storm, the Kosovo air campaign, or the war against the Taliban, with far fewer air, sea, and ground forces. Moreover, as the events of September 11 indicated, we will also encounter adversaries who will not line up tanks in the desert, as they did in the past. In the future, potential enemies will use high-tech weapons such as sophisticated missiles and information warfare against American and allied forces—and our military must be prepared to counter them. We can maintain our edge over these future challenges by recasting our forces now, while we have the time and resources to do it.

The plan I propose tonight will achieve this objective in several ways:

- Redirects our research and development priorities by emphasizing these new technologies.

- Takes special measures to safeguard systems crucial to the warfare of the future, so that the United States is not at risk of suffering a surprise technological strike that could cripple our information, communications, and computer networks.

- Reshapes our forces to free up resources for innovation and to reflect the new ways of warfare.

I want to explain to you now just what threats we face, how the revolution in military affairs can deal with these threats, and the changes that we need to make.

Our defense planning begins with the definition of our interests and the threats to them. The twentieth century taught Americans that what we value most—our democratic freedoms—can be put at risk by events far from our shores. We also learned that our prosperity depends on a peaceful world.

We have therefore made enormous sacrifices in lives, as well as in monetary and material wealth, to preserve our democracy—indeed, to give democracy a fighting chance in the rest of the world. And in this we have essentially succeeded. After two world wars, a third called the Cold War, the war against al Qaeda and the Taliban in Afghanistan, and numerous other conflicts, the United States remains secure and prosperous today.

The world, however, is neither settled nor entirely peaceful. Newspapers and television remind us that dangerous dictators are still at work, that states break up in civil or ethnic strife, and that terrorists seek to undermine any states that work for freedom in the world.

Along the lines of traditional threats, we are working to incorporate former adversaries, such as Russia and China, into a more cooperative international system, but we do not yet know whether their experiments in political and economic reform will result in prosperous, stable democracies. As for new, asymmetrical threats, there is an increasing probability that weapons of mass destruction—nuclear, chemical, or biological—may be acquired by certain evil states or terrorists.

Still, on balance, we are much less threatened today by any other nation than we were only a few short years ago. The nuclear arsenals of Russia are being reduced significantly. No major power in Europe or Asia will be able to challenge us militarily for some time. The axis of evil states know very well not to contest us in major warfare, thanks to Operation Desert Storm, although in the future we can expect them to probe our weaknesses rather than array themselves against our strengths, as Saddam Hussein did in 1991.

Some would argue that this situation furnishes a basis for massive defense cuts or at least confidence in our long-term security from traditional threats. If we have any challenge, however, it is complacency. The hard-won efforts of previous generations have given us the precious gift of time—time to look ahead and prepare for the military problems of the future.

War today wears many faces, from the sophisticated technician preparing the electronic guidance of advanced missiles to the fanatic in the streets armed with dime-store explosives to the terrorist who turns a civilian airliner into a lethal weapon. War in the future may be the silent action of weapons in space, the hum of computers selecting targets, and the surprise of a technological strike against satellites or computers when one side discovers itself blinded and unable to either locate the enemy or communicate with its own forces.

Potential future adversaries will most likely reject the example of Saddam Hussein, who foolishly arrayed his large armored forces against us in an open desert. Rather, our future enemies, like the terrorist leader Osama bin Laden, will seek to exploit their strengths against American weaknesses: they will attempt to deny the United States the use of overseas bases by attacking them with chemical or biological weapons; they will prevent the buildup of large American ground forces abroad by hitting key supply areas and transportation hubs with cheap ballistic missiles like the Scud; they will attack our large aircraft carriers with inexpensive antiship cruise missiles and cheap sea mines; they will combat our multi-million-dollar aircraft with accurate ground-to-air missiles that cost only a few thousand dollars; and they will attempt to disrupt our communications and intelligence networks that rely so heavily on advanced automation and computerization.

To combat these new tactics, the United States must create a technologically advanced force that is mobile, stealthy, and agile, and that can attack targets from great distances. Such a force will not need huge forward bases or bulky supply lines, as it will be able to attack targets anywhere with a variety of sea-, space-, air-, or ground-based weapons. This is a very different force from the lethal, yet in many areas still ponderous, military we have today.

When the Cold War ended, we possessed the world's most powerful military, with unmatched nuclear and conventional forces, a global reach, and advanced technology. The war in the Persian Gulf showed what we could do. Since then, we have reduced our military overall by one-third. I fully support that decision, which reflected both lesser threats and America's need to put its fiscal house in order. But that still leaves us with forces designed 30 years ago primarily for a Cold War conflict in Europe that ended more than a decade ago. As a result, we are poorly prepared to exploit the next wave of technological innovation and use it to successfully combat the threats of the future. Too much of our defense policy is mere tinkering with an increasingly obsolete structure that we cannot afford and do not need. Too much energy and investment is focused on being ready to fight two nearly simultaneous regional conflicts, the prospects of which are becoming increasingly unlikely. By attempting to keep in readiness a military intended to meet the least likely event—a conventional war—we courted instead a more likely disaster, a 21st-century Pearl Harbor from a terrorist group or adversarial state using technology to attack us where we are weak. Al Qaeda terrorists were able to attack the World Trade Center and the Pentagon because the military-technological revolution is available to anyone who seeks to take advantage of it, including terrorist groups and other potential adversaries. Next time we may experience a 21st-century Hiroshima if these terrorists or one of the axis of evil states obtains a weapon of mass destruction.

But for all this talk about the revolution in military affairs, what exactly is it?

THE MILITARY-TECHNOLOGICAL REVOLUTION

The first step to success on the battlefield is to know the adversary: to understand his capabilities and intentions, to know where he is, what he is doing, and the identity of his forces. The second step is to defeat the enemy through superior tactics, maneuvers, and firepower. Until recently, all military efforts concentrated on creating ever greater force and explosive power, the most spectacular example being the nuclear weapon. This effort required the mobilization of whole societies and, throughout the Cold War, the danger of nuclear holocaust.

But what if much of this is no longer necessary? What if we could locate the enemy precisely, strike him accurately from a very long distance, and do so with a minimum of force? What if a network of sensors deployed on the ground, in the sea, in the air, and in space could pinpoint enemy movements with unerring accuracy? What, then, if computers could instantaneously process this information and relay it to a network of weapons that could launch and guide precision munitions toward the enemy targets—with little danger to U.S. forces, who will no longer have to meet their enemy face to face? These prospects are what the military-technological revolution is all about: the increasingly precise knowledge of the target's location and the increasingly accurate fire that can be brought against it from long range.

This is the same technological revolution that has given Americans unprecedented access to information across greater distances with lightning speed. Now, it can also give our defense forces unparalleled precision in finding and hitting the target. This "what if" world is already with us. Indeed, we saw elements of this in the war in Afghanistan. Let me give you a few other examples:

- The World War I telegraph, the fastest transmitter of data in its day, sent 30 words a minute; Teletype increased this rate to 66 words a minute by the early 1970s. Computers used in Operation Desert Storm in 1991, by comparison, processed 192,000 bits of information per minute. We can look forward to processing millions—even a trillion—bits of information per minute as computer chips become more sophisticated. The trend is clearly toward even faster and smaller computers.

- During the Persian Gulf War, one F-117 stealth fighter with laser-guided bombs destroyed the same type of targets that it took 1,500 B-17 missions in World War II and 176 F-4 missions in Vietnam to destroy. Those same F-117s struck 40 percent of Iraq's strategic targets with only 2 percent of our total aircraft sorties.

- In the Gulf War, the United States had to deploy 10 aircraft to be sure of taking out a single target. In the war in Afghanistan, the United States budgeted two targets per aircraft.

- In the war in Afghanistan, Tomahawk land-attack cruise missiles and unmanned planes were able to find their marks with no risk to our forces.

- During the Gulf War and the war in Afghanistan, our space-based navigation satellites enabled allied forces to maneuver precisely across trackless desert.

- In the Kosovo conflict, long-range B-2 bombers from the United States flew 2 percent of the missions but delivered 11 percent of the bombs. In Afghanistan, long-range bombers flew 10 percent of the missions but delivered 70 percent of the bombs.

- In the war in Afghanistan, the use of precision-guided munitions, which were 90 percent effective, increased to 60 percent from only 7 percent in the Gulf War.

In short, new ways to locate the enemy precisely, to react rapidly, and to strike accurately are already transforming warfare as we know it. But we must be aware that this transformation works both ways. The key to battle is not only the possession and use of information but the denial of it to others.

And that is why I used the phrase "a 21st century Pearl Harbor." We are not the only ones exploring the frontiers of high technology.

You must know, as I do, that even inexpensive missiles are already accurate enough to threaten $100 million aircraft and billion-dollar ships. You must know, as I do, that systems already exist that would deny our forces some of the advantages that made the Gulf War, the Kosovo air war, and the war in Afghanistan such massive successes with so few casualties. An adversary need not build a huge and expensive military to challenge the United States today. A modest investment in weapons of mass destruction, short-range ballistic missiles, and many high-tech weapons can be effective in denying American forces access to areas such as the Persian Gulf, Central Asia, or the Taiwan Straits. If our military forces are not prepared to combat these threats with information-age technology, they could suffer many casualties against a relatively unsophisticated enemy.

The long, sad history of warfare gives many examples of how victorious nations became complacent and then suffered catastrophic results. In the last century, it was the victors of World War I who invented the tank, only to be crushed by the tank blitzkrieg of 1940. The German tanks used in World War II were not that much superior to those of the French or Soviets, but the Germans understood how they could revolutionize warfare by putting those tanks to new use: to attack. The victims had expected simply to fight the old way, even with new equipment.

The lessons are plain enough. We cannot prepare for yesterday's battles without risking the loss of tomorrow's wars. We cannot base our confidence solely on our ability to invent ever more sophisticated versions of the weapons used in past battles. We must instead use new weapons in new ways, with new organization and new tactics, if we are to prevail next time.

I am therefore proposing the transformation of our defense through a revolutionary seven-point plan.

A SEVEN-POINT PLAN

1. Accelerate Research and Development Spending to Reflect the New Priorities.
Our objective is to bring the new technologies of location, reaction, and accuracy on-line as fast as possible. I propose, therefore, to increase research and development spending over the next decade, instead of keeping it level as currently planned. We should make a $500 billion investment focused on emerging technologies, such as:

- Weapon systems that can strike more precisely and at greater ranges;

- Smaller, more mobile computers and communications systems that enable us to make better and faster decisions and to maneuver more quickly;

- Information-warfare technologies that can cripple an adversary's command, control, communications, and computer facilities while protecting our own;

- Stealth technologies and techniques that make our forces harder to see and therefore less vulnerable to attack;

- Unmanned vehicles and robots that reduce the risks to our soldiers, sailors, airmen, and marines;

- New platforms for submerged power projection and undersea warfare; and

- Space-based systems that can not only support ground, sea, and air forces with better intelligence, communications, navigation, and weather forecasting but also deliver firepower anywhere in the world on a moment's notice, including against ballistic missiles launched at the United States.

2. Take Special Measures to Protect the Key Elements of the Military Revolution.
America's defenses will also include an ability to deploy robust space-warfare capabilities and independent, integrated information-warfare capabilities. This will ensure that our nation never suffers a space or information strike such as a crippling computer virus for which we are not prepared.

3. Reduce Our Planned Force Structure Over a Decade.
This reduction has two purposes: to free up resources and to create the new defense we need. We will gradually eliminate some Army divisions, tactical fighter wings, carrier battle groups, and the Air Force's older B-1 and B-52 bombers and strategic nuclear missiles. Systems and units that were originally fielded to fight the massive campaigns of the Cold War will be phased out. We will also reopen with Congress the issue of reducing the size of the Marine Corps below its congressionally mandated level of three divisions and three air wings.

Why cut down the force size when preparing to meet new threats? Because the reorganization of our remaining forces into new units that fully exploit advanced technologies and new war-fighting concepts will more than offset their reduction in size.

As a result of these and other changes, the armed forces will be gradually reduced over the next decade to about 1 million people, compared to the 1.45 million we have today. The National Guard reserve forces will also be cut by a commensurate amount. To ease the strain on the remaining troops, our forward-deployed forces in Europe will be reduced from 100,000 to 20,000. The cutback in this expensive force structure will free up the money we will need to revolutionize our military and to pay the remaining troops a wage that is sufficient to compete with the private sector and provide them with the quality of life they deserve.

4. Develop a New Strategic Framework.
Just as there is a revolution in military affairs, there must also be a revolution in our strategic nuclear affairs. More than a decade after the end of the Cold War, both the doctrine of mutually assured destruction and the Anti-Ballistic Missile (ABM) Treaty are outmoded. We are no longer threatened by Russian missiles but by missiles in the hands of outlaw states like Iraq and North Korea. Russian President Vladimir Putin and I acknowledged these changes when we agreed in Moscow in May 2002 to reduce each of our countries' strategic offensive nuclear weapons from 6,000 to between 1,700 and 2,200. My administration took a further step out of the shackles of history when we withdrew from the ABM Treaty in June 2002, having given Russia the proper notice.

Now, freed from the ABM Treaty's constraints, we can actually have the first stage of a robust national missile defense system in place by 2004.

I will also let the Chinese leadership know that our national missile defense deployment is not directed against their country. I will tell them that the United States will have no objection to their plan to modernize and enhance their limited strategic offensive capability.

5. Maintain Superiority in Space So That We Can Ensure Its Use on Our Own Terms.

In the Persian Gulf War, the Kosovo conflict, and the war against the Taliban, we achieved our objectives quickly and decisively with a minimum of casualties because of our ability to use our orbiting satellites to guide our weapons to their targets. But we cannot assume that this capability will remain unchallenged. At present there are 1,000 active satellites orbiting the earth. About 125 of these, or 12 percent, belong to the U.S. military. Within a decade, that percentage will diminish as the number of satellites in space will double. As the Space Commission report of January 2001 noted, "every medium—air, land and sea—has seen conflict. Reality indicates space will be no different."

To ensure that we maintain our dominance in space, we are significantly expanding our expenditures on offensive and defensive space assets. These increased funds will go toward space sensors, space-based radars, and anti-satellite weaponry.

6. Refocus Our Forces Toward Dealing With Conflict in Asia.

The relative importance of Asia to our security is growing, particularly as the risk of major war in Europe shrinks to practically zero. Several flashpoints across Asia are of particular concern to us: the Korean Peninsula, where the North Korean regime continues to be unpredictable despite recent discussions with South Korea; the conflict between India and Pakistan over Kashmir, which became even more dangerous with those countries' acquisition of nuclear weapons, as we saw in the spring of 2002. The question of Taiwan and China; the instability of Indonesia; and the contested claims by several countries on the Spratly Islands in the South China Sea. We must be prepared to protect our interests and security should any of these potential conflicts deteriorate further. To do this, we will rely on our European allies to do more on their continent with less American involvement.

7. Make Homeland Defense a Priority of the Armed Forces.

As we saw on September 11, 2001, the U.S. homeland itself is vulnerable to devastating attack. Therefore, we have some portion of our forces organized and equipped to deal with this new form

[55]

of warfare. Although ultimate responsibility for homeland defense will not lie with the armed forces, they will play a crucial role in carrying out this mission. To ensure that they can do this, the Department of Defense will establish the Northern Command in October 2002.

THE NEW U.S. MILITARY

Once the transformation of our forces is complete, the United States will field the most advanced and effective military in the world, one truly up to the task of defending this nation's interests and objectives well into this century. Instead of the currently large, heavy forces designed to engage in direct and costly combat primarily in Europe, we will emphasize long-range precision weapons and control of information to disrupt and overcome an adversary's ability to wage war.

For strategic missions, we will rely on a nuclear deterrent of 1,700–2,200 warheads rather than the current arsenal of 6,000, and we will work with Russia to see if we can bring that number even lower. These weapons of strategic warfare will be bolstered substantially by two other elements: first, our ability to carry out multidimensional, long-range precision strikes; and second, our capacity to wage information warfare. Together, these three capabilities will comprise a new strategic triad that replaces the old, purely nuclear arsenal. As our technological work progresses on the non-nuclear parts of this triad, we will be able to reduce our stock of nuclear weapons gradually without any danger to the United States and without losing the effectiveness of our deterrent.

Our conventional forces will also be much changed. The Army and the Marine Corps should include no more than 30 information-intensive regiments and brigades. These smaller and more lethal units will also be mobile and stealthy in their own way. Some ground forces will focus specifically on combat in cities and towns, a growing need in an increasingly urbanized world, and will use robots and other advanced technologies to minimize casualties in urban operations. The Army's ground forces will be deployed principally by air and able to conduct decisive close-combat and land-based, deep-strike operations anywhere in the world. Forward-deployed forces will be reduced substantially, and the marines will rely on smaller sea-based forces that emphasize stand-off weapons and unmanned aerial vehicles. This force will be capable of operating anywhere in the world with no need for local bases.

Our Air Force will evolve into a Space and Air Force and we will combine the space and strategic commands into a single command with global reach. Aircraft of the future will be stealthier, be able to carry more precision weapons, fly longer distances, and be increasingly unmanned—a move that will both lower cost and raise performance over piloted aircraft. Our Navy will begin to shift away from a carrier-based force to one that provides the same sort of mobile sea power through craft such as the Arsenal ship, the Stealth battleship, the distributed-warfare capital ship, and the small Streetfighter ships. All these concepts use advances in information technology, stealth, and precision munitions to spread increased naval firepower among many different and smaller ships. The large aircraft carrier, manned by more than 5,000 sailors, is a magnificent vessel, but it is expensive to operate and increasingly easy to find—and thus vulnerable to cheap anti-ship missiles and torpedoes. The war in Afghanistan gave an indication of this reality: carrier aircraft flew 75 percent of the sorties in the first four months of the conflict, but they dropped less than 30 percent of the weapons.

Finally, our reserve forces will operate unmanned aerial vehicles, micro-robots, and satellites; pilot transport aircraft; perform information-warfare, network-management, and distributed-logistics functions in direct support of our active forces; and reinforce active forces in other combat and combat-support areas. As the National Security Strategy Group report of March 2001 recommended, the National Guard will be given homeland security as its primary mission. Accordingly, its heavy, Cold War–era combat divisions will be eliminated. I intend the innovation of our forces to apply to all forces, not just active-duty units.

Finally, we cannot have a revolutionary change in our field forces without some similar movement in the Pentagon itself. Our current organizational structure for national defense is a relic from 1947. I have therefore directed the secretary of defense to apply the same kind of innovative thinking to our defense bureaucracy as he plans for our fighting forces. Because technological innovation obscures the traditional boundaries between air, sea, and ground, perhaps we no longer need services organized along those lines. In an era when a stealth submarine can effectively engage enemy tanks or an army might have many assets based in space, does it still make sense to separate the training of our services or count our strength in ground divisions, air wings, and navy carrier battle groups? In the digital age, when corporations are flattening hierarchies and sharing information across work groups, can the Pentagon afford to keep its large and unwieldy organizational structure? Is our government, split as it is into various agencies with their separate responsibilities, even organized in the right way for information warfare? These are just some of the issues I would like to pursue with the same energy that we will use to remake our fighting units.

And here is some good news. We can acquire this revolutionary military force with a defense budget of approximately $400 billion per year, using the reductions in force structure and cancellation of new legacy systems like the F-22 and the Crusader to give us the extra funding we need for both the new procurements and the additional research and development. For example, for the cost of a single F-22 we can buy five unmanned Predator aircraft.

My fellow Americans, I realize that this plan contains its share of risks. Technological innovation is always a gamble. There could be delays. A program of such magnitude usually takes more time and money than we expect. A smaller force may not be able to respond as robustly to situations such as that in Kosovo. Moreover, we are deliberately discarding forces that worked for us in the past.

I am also aware that revolutions upset traditional structures and discard time-tested arrangements that have served us well. The real impediments to change are often more psychological than physical.

Although we should not let psychological barriers stop us, neither should we underestimate these difficulties, three of which deserve special attention:

1. The current "Cold War lite" force structure will not go quietly into the night. We have managed to reduce our operating forces very successfully since the early 1990s, only to take on various peacekeeping duties that have imposed considerable strain. Yet while fewer than 130,000 sailors run the entire Atlantic Fleet, about 150,000 military and civilian personnel are assigned to the Washington, D.C., area to manage the military. I was astonished to learn that figure, and I know you are too. We are going to use a heavy hand to eliminate unnecessary layers of command and management.

2. The education of our military still reflects the old emphasis on hierarchies and separate services. We have taken great strides toward joint operations in recent years, but we still need greater emphasis on functional frameworks from the outset.

   As in Afghanistan, where Army Special Forces provided target information to Air Force and Navy aircraft, joint operations between our services should be the first, not the last, choice.

3. The United States and its allies are entering this revolution together, and we should begin to plan and train as coalitions, not wait until a crisis forces us to look at a problem together. However, our allies are not launching into the military-technological revolution with the same enthusiasm as we are. To keep systems compatible so that we can work together on the battlefield, I will redouble our efforts to bring our partners, particularly our NATO allies, along in this endeavor, especially in the area of missile defense.

As we work to overcome these problems, we can expect a good deal of controversy and uncertainty. Some will argue that the risks are too great, others that the obstacles cannot be overcome. Honest differences of opinion will arise over whether the technologies can work. I have already noted that our plans are based on a strategic estimate that rules out a large, Cold War–scale security threat for the better part of a decade, and some will see in this a serious error.

To those critics I say: Yes, we will still need some contingency capabilities; we will still be sending some old-fashioned forces to deal with some old-fashioned problems. And yes, American soldiers, marines, sailors, and airmen will still be going in harm's way.

There is no avoiding the hard and brutal fact that war is about death. As one young officer said, "this modernization debate is only about budgets and bureaucratic turf if you don't have to go to war; for people who actually have to go to war, it's about living or dying." We can do our best to deter; but deterrence may still fail, and we must still prevail. We will prevail because we are and will remain far superior to any potential adversary.

Ultimately, the defense of the United States is in the hands of those Americans who volunteer to defend us. I have a special message to those men and women of our armed services. The plan I put forward tonight may fill you with questions and lead you to doubt the future. Yet its purpose is in fact to secure the future. You who have studied war know better than I or your fellow citizens that the revolution in military affairs is not an option but a fast-dawning reality. You on whom the burden falls to defend us with your lives know better than any other Americans the potential of this revolution and the peril in pretending we can avoid it. And it is because of my confidence in your capacity to make the changes successfully that I have decided to pursue such a revolutionary defense policy.

There is yet more to be said at this time to you, the American people. I have described several challenges to our national security tonight, chief among them, perhaps, a complacency about the future. I have said that the threats can be met by reordering our defense to accord with the new revolution so that we may field forces better able to find and strike our adversaries, using the minimum power necessary to defeat him and providing the maximum protection of American lives in the process. I have also put forward a plan to pay for this reordering which balances the risks.

Yet we know our own history. Like many nations, we were alerted to our deficiencies in defense only after suffering disaster, as we did on September 11. In the absence of a clear and present danger in the last decade, it was easier to drift along, secure in the memories of past triumphs. This drift, and this alone, is in fact the clear and present danger.

I ask you tonight, therefore, to apply to our national security the same sense of alertness and adventure that distinguishes our civilian society. From the beginning of this republic, observers have been struck by America's eagerness to embrace change, our pride in revolutionary advances, and our ability to remake our world even in the absence of any pressing need to do so. It is this high confidence that has made the United States the world's leader. And that is why I am so confident that with your support, we can embrace this revolution in military affairs and by doing so, secure our future.

SPEECH THREE: AN EVOLUTIONARY
TRANSFORMATION

A plan to keep a slightly smaller military focused on near-term challenges (such as fighting the war on terrorism) and prepared to meet many different threats, ranging from deterring the axis of evil states to peacekeeping in failed states, while continuing to innovate and modernize—and all within a $400 billion budget that will be adjusted annually for inflation.

Members of Congress and My Fellow Americans:

Thank you for welcoming me to Capitol Hill this evening. As you remember from my appearance before you on September 20, 2001, it has long been customary for presidents to address Congress directly in times of emergency or to advocate change. But I have decided to speak to you tonight for a different reason. I am asking you to support continuity, to stay the course in American defense policy. The reason is simple: only by pursuing our current course, which, as we have seen in Afghanistan, has given us the best-equipped, best-trained, and best-led military forces in the entire world, can we defend American security in the most prudent way.

In this new century, aggression by a single, powerful adversary no longer threatens the United States. Nonetheless, we still face a series of dangerous uncertainties. The United States and its allies could be menaced by another act of terrorism, the attack of a rogue or evil state, or, over the longer term, the appearance of a major rival. You also know that in the last decade our forces have been deeply engaged in war-fighting and peacekeeping missions to secure order and hope in countries suffering from civil war and collapsed governments; as I speak to you tonight, U.S. forces are deployed in Afghanistan, the Philippines, and the Balkans. We therefore need a flexible balance of forces to deal with these contingencies, forces designed according to a plan that realistically assesses the threats and apportions our resources carefully between current operations and future needs. And we had this balance in the 1990s.

But now some want to change our spending priorities and overall strategy in a revolutionary way.

You may have heard or read that our military is too small, or that we are spending much too little, or that our forces are overextended. Other complaints allege that we are missing a technological revolution that will leave us with an obsolete defense. And yet another commonly heard claim is that we are still spending at Cold War levels and therefore can reduce our defense spending by as much as 20 percent.

These ideas all arise from the same mistake: they pay too much attention to a single problem at the cost of neglecting the others. Those who would spend more money fail to focus on the receding dangers of major attacks in the Persian Gulf or Asia, rely on misleading comparisons about the shares of GDP or the percentage of the federal budget devoted to defense, or exaggerate the number of our forces involved in peacekeeping and the cost of such missions. In addition, they ignore the fact that since 1998, defense spending has actually been increasing in real terms. The fiscal year 2003 budget, which was enacted by Congress, contains a real increase of about 10 percent, the largest jump since the Reagan-era buildup. (In fact, over the past two years defense spending has increased by almost 20 percent in real terms.) The advocates of the revolution in military affairs would hazard U.S. defense by embracing weapons, organizations, and tactics that are best approached in a gradual "prove as you go" fashion. Finally, we would risk our credibility abroad and invite a hostile challenge if we made further huge reductions in the size and deployments of our forces or in defense spending.

We are not going to make these mistakes, particularly at this juncture. We are not going to increase spending on the wrong forces, and we are not going to abandon necessary peacekeeping missions. We are not going to risk our security with a roll of the technological dice. And we are certainly not going to jeopardize our international leadership and vital national interests with a dangerous downsizing of our armed forces.

STAYING THE COURSE

Instead, we are going to stay the course and evolve. Naturally, I am not promising you the moon at little or no cost. There are trade-offs that I shall explain later. The evolutionary approach I propose, however, provides for an efficient defense and gives us the flexibility to adjust our course when necessary. Part of my purpose in speaking to you is also to outline a few of those adjustments that will continue to give us the forces we need. These include:

- Greater emphasis on proven technological and organizational innovations that make our current forces more effective;

- Increased attention to homeland defense;

- Increased procurement of new and replacement equipment to prepare for the future; and

- More effective spending of our resources through the reduction of overhead and the privatization of more support functions.

Achieving these objectives is the best investment we can make for our future.

Let me begin with the most basic issue in planning our defense: our interests and the threats to those interests. The twentieth century taught Americans that what we value most—our democratic freedoms—can be put at risk by events far from our shores. And these events can also threaten our prosperity. Today, we have trading relationships with Europe, the Middle East, and Asia that are vital to the health of the U.S. economy. Since 1970, the percentage of our GDP derived from international trade has more than tripled and is still rising. Instability in one area of the world could easily spread. Our military should be regarded not only as the defender of our democracy but also as the shield of our prosperity.

Unfortunately, as we saw on September 11, the end of the Cold War did not mean the end of trouble in the world, either for others or for ourselves. Although we are now naturally focused on the war on terrorism, let me discuss briefly a few of the other problems we face abroad that could menace our interests.

The "Axis of Evil"

North Korea is on the brink of starvation and without allies. Yet despite the fact that the regime has begun talking to South Korea, it remains armed to the teeth, its troops poised to invade its southern neighbor. In the Persian Gulf, Iraq still possesses enough conventional military power and chemical and biological weapons to threaten its neighbors in the absence of U.S. air, sea, and land power. Iran, a supporter of terrorism, seeks nuclear and other weapons of mass destruction and the ballistic missiles to deliver them. To protect our interests and our allies from this axis of evil, we must have forces capable of deterring aggression—and if deterrence fails, of fighting and winning wars—nearly simultaneously in Northeast Asia and in the Middle East. In this new century, however, we can accomplish this mission with less force than in the recent past.

Collapsing Nations

We live in a revolutionary era when the international economy and global communications have raised expectations of shared prosperity around the world. But not every nation has been able to deal successfully with such changes. Some countries have buckled and broken down into savage civil wars. Bewildered peoples, frightened by demagogues, have sought safety once more in the doctrines of racial hatred and ethnic cleansing that we hoped had been consigned to the dustbin of history. These threats to international order challenge our fundamental values and sometimes our national interests, because the spread of such doctrines would negate the peaceful, democratic, cooperative world we have worked so hard to achieve. We must therefore be able to act militarily where necessary, whether in cooperation with other nations or unilaterally, to restore peace, order, and hope. And we must do this without undermining our ability to swiftly defeat two aggressors at one time.

The Nuclear Threat and Weapons of Mass Destruction

The end of the Cold War means that we need no longer fear a nuclear war that could end civilization. But huge arsenals still exist, and violent and irresponsible leaders or terrorists might yet acquire nuclear weapons. Worse still, we may well see chemical or biological weapons in the wrong hands, mounted on missiles capable of reaching the United States. Those who might be tempted to challenge us in this way must know that American preemption or retaliation would be swift, sure, and devastating, and that we will continue our efforts to develop an effective defense against these weapons. The danger is especially acute when it comes from terrorists, who will increasingly have access to these weapons, and who might use not missiles but instead planes, suitcases, or small ships to deliver them.

Potential Rivals in Europe or Asia

We are free today of a major international rival. Russia is going through wrenching political and economic change. In Asia, U.S. policy is to foster constructive relations with China, the world's most populous nation, which is also engaged in a profound transformation. But the outcome of these unprecedented experiments is uncertain, and in the meantime, the NATO countries, Japan, and our other friends and allies must be able to rely on the presence of American forces to sustain secure and cooperative relationships across old Cold War boundaries. Indeed, the very commitment of those forces supports our diplomacy as we expand NATO to increase security in Europe, and as we encourage both Russia and China to join an international community they once opposed. Significant numbers of forward-deployed American forces are therefore still essential to the overall security of both Europe and Asia. We will continue to maintain these forces and, with the continued financial support of the countries that host them, can absorb the incurred costs in the current defense budget.

CHANGES WE HAVE MADE

Since the end of the Cold War, we have been very aware of these contingencies , and we have rebalanced and reshaped the Cold War–era military to deal with them. We have retained our basic strategy:

to secure our interests, we must be able to deter, preempt, and defeat challenges to our security at home and in Europe, Asia, and the Middle East. And in the 2001 Quadrennial Defense Review, we retained a basic benchmark for our military capabilities: we must be able to deal with major crises in more than one region nearly simultaneously. At the same time, we have recognized that the diminishing potential challenges from rogue states allow us to achieve our objectives with smaller forces and at much lower cost.

If, for instance, we were to respond again to aggression from Saddam Hussein or bring about regime change in Iraq, we could do so with much less force than in 1991. While we have decreased our forces by more than one-third since the Gulf War, the battles of Operation Desert Storm reduced the military might of the Iraqi Army and Air Force by an even greater proportion. Similarly, a less-threatening situation prevails on the Korean Peninsula, where the forces of our ally South Korea greatly outclass those of the regime in the impoverished north.

I recognize that it may appear unrealistic to expect smaller American forces to fight and win against two aggressors simultaneously. It may also seem unlikely that two such conflicts would happen at once. Our strategy therefore will center on deterrence of critical threats and on being able to respond effectively to nearly simultaneous crises around the globe. Through the use of airpower and in conjunction with our regional allies, we can deter or halt aggression until we can mobilize the ground forces needed to win a decisive victory in any theater. This new military, which will also be prepared for playing its part in the war on terrorism, as well as peacekeeping and other operations in places such as Bosnia and Kosovo, will be an effective, albeit smaller, force for a more efficient American strategy.

Many Americans do not realize the enormous changes that have already taken place, especially our effort to reduce unnecessary defense expenditures. Let me give you a few figures:

- In the 1980s, we spent almost $400 billion, in current dollars, per year on defense; in the 1990s, we spent about $325 billion a year.

- In 1989, defense took 28 percent of the federal budget; today it takes 16 percent.

- In 1989, defense took 6 percent of our GDP; today it takes about 3.5 percent.

Reductions in active-duty personnel have been even more significant, from 2.2 million in 1989 to 1.45 million at the end of 2001. About 200,000 U.S. troops are deployed overseas now, compared with 500,000 in 1989. Our defense industry has also been transformed. Instead of 3.7 million workers and a $120 billion yearly procurement budget, today the defense sector employs about 2 million workers, and the procurement budget is $60 billion.

I do not regret these reductions, for nothing hurts our security and our economic health more than a huge waste of resources. Americans should also applaud the way our forces have adapted to their new conditions. Our soldiers, sailors, marines, and airmen have retained their readiness, spirit, and "can do" attitude despite increased deployments and decreased budgets. As we saw in Afghanistan, today's armed services consist of highly trained professionals, capable of dominating the battle on land, at sea, and in the air. We are the leaders in using space for communications, navigation, intelligence, and many other functions. And we have preeminent nuclear forces.

Now the time has come for a further rearrangement of our defense to give it the shape we need for the future. We know that if the tires on our cars are just slightly out of line, the tires themselves will eventually be ruined. Today, our defense posture is slightly out of line. By correcting it now, we will spare ourselves a lot of damage later.

As we reduced the size of the military and reshaped it over the last decade, we hedged against the uncertainties of the post–Cold War era by emphasizing readiness and operations over research, investment, and procurement. These proportions must now be altered to adequately equip our forces for the future.

A SIX-POINT PLAN

I am happy to report that we can make these changes with a budget of approximately $400 billion that will increase only at the pace of inflation. And we can do it without upsetting the careful balance of forces that allows us to deal with the full range of potential threats.

I am therefore proposing a six-point plan for an evolutionary transformation of our defense posture. This plan will sustain our ability to deal with simultaneous challenges to American interests in more than one region while preparing our forces for the threats of the future through new emphasis on research, investment, and procurement.

1. Carefully Pursue Technological Innovation.

Although I have warned against a full-fledged commitment to any revolutionary technologies that are largely unproven, we must increase our emphasis on tried-and-true technological advances, especially those that enhance our capabilities in communications, intelligence, and space. We will need to protect our military and commercial satellites from attack or disruption by an adversary. High-tech forces that wage war from a greater distance require more targeting data, precise navigational information, and the rapid distribution of information. Advances in these fields can also facilitate timely identification of missile launches, a key element in our continuing program to develop missile defenses.

2. Continue to Increase Our Procurement.

Procurement of new equipment has been too slow for too long. The Department of Defense was two years late in reaching the Joint Chiefs of Staff's recommended level of $60 billion a year for procurement; therefore, we will increase spending for new weapons to $70 billion within two years. This does not mean, however, that we will buy unnecessary weapons. For example, our warplanes and warships so outclass the competition that we do not need to procure large numbers of newer systems beyond those currently planned. Technological advances will also enable us to reduce the size of active-duty forces slightly while still retaining much of their firepower. This means smaller units in all the services that can do more with less manpower.

3. Manage the Department of Defense More Efficiently.

To meet our needs without increasing the overall budget means we must tackle long overdue reforms. One is to close surplus bases. Just look at the numbers: force structures and manpower are down 37 percent since the end of the Cold War, but base structures are down only 25 percent worldwide and 20 percent in the United States. Dealing forthrightly with this issue can save at least $3.5 billion a year for the taxpayers. I know that this is a tough issue for Congress, but it is an even tougher issue to deny our troops what they need. To save even more, we will privatize more of the Pentagon's maintenance and support functions. The Defense Reform Initiative of 1998 estimated that $10 billion could be saved this way. Privatization is worth the effort, even if the savings turn out to be slightly less.

4. Modernize the Compensation System.

We currently pay certain military personnel too much and others not enough. The Defense Department needs to move from a one-size-fits-all system to one that rewards performance, not just longevity. The current retirement system gives us the worst of all possible worlds: it is very expensive but does not achieve its objective of retaining the best people. A defined contribution system with earlier vesting, similar to the system used for federal civil servants, will save $5 billion a year and retain the right people for the appropriate amount of time. Moreover, we will increase the housing allowance for those military people living off base to reflect the changes in the civilian market. Finally, we will also turn over construction and maintenance of on-base housing to the private sector and allow the dependents of military personnel and retirees to enroll in the federal employee health benefits program.

5. Rotate and Deploy Our Troops.

As you may know from many reports, the repeated deployments of our military have strained the force. I am convinced that we do not need to have either a larger or more expensive force. But to alleviate this damaging strain on our people and our equipment, we must manage our existing force with greater efficiency. A new system of rotating overseas deployments will let a slightly smaller force take on all of today's security challenges with no dent in readiness or morale.

6. Make Homeland Defense the Primary Mission of the National Guard.

As we learned from the events of September 11, our own country is now vulnerable to an attack by terrorists with global reach. Employing the resources of the Army and Air National Guard, in tandem with the CIA, the FBI, the Immigration and Naturalization Service, and state and local officials should help prevent or cope with another terrorist attack.

All told, these changes in force structure and organization will allow us to reduce the U.S. military from the current 1.45 million active-duty troops to about 1.3 million by 2003. The reserve forces will be cut from 864,000 to 700,000 troops.

These measures can save the Department of Defense up to $10 billion per year. The money will fund the procurement of new and replacement weapon systems, although I propose cutting back on the planned purchases of certain tactical aircraft, submarines, and ships.

This program for an evolutionary transformation also avoids serious errors that could badly damage our military, and with it our national security, over the long haul. Some people, for example, think a large military means more security. They are wrong. Keeping a force structure larger than what we need actually weakens our defense in the long term because it diverts resources from necessary investments, whether in procurement, training, or research. We do not face today a fundamental security threat from Russia, China, or elsewhere, and we do not need to build up an additional force structure to deal with a potential rival a decade or more away.

Others, alarmed by the complexities of peacekeeping, argue that we should abandon this necessary responsibility. The critics of our peacekeeping missions offer a seductive argument: Would we not be better off simply concentrating on waging the war on terrorism and deterring the axis of evil states, reducing the residual nuclear threat, and sustaining our alliances in Asia and Europe? Can't others, our allies or the United Nations, do the peacekeeping job?

My answer to this is yes, we most definitely should call on our allies and friends, as we have done in Afghanistan, and even the United Nations, to help. But you know, as I do, that when all is said and done, their efforts alone will not be enough to protect our interests, advance our values, or defend our security. What's more, these peacekeeping operations have accounted for only about 2 percent of our defense expenditures over the past decade.

The post–Cold War world and our hopes for a better international order are being put to the test by terrorists with global reach who thrive where they can find collapsing states, civil strife, ethnic hatred, and all the other situations that have required peacekeeping. This is not simply a humanitarian issue, although humanitarian relief itself is a compelling reason to act. We must think of the impact that cumulative inaction has on our strategy of deterring terrorism and aggression. We avert our eyes from this peacekeeping obligation only at greater peril. Surely the lesson of the last century is that those with evil in their hearts see the failings of good men and women in lesser crises as a sign of deeper and more dangerous flaws.

Make no mistake. Having won the Cold War, we must now win the peace. The prospects for that peace depend upon the United States. Our wisdom, our will, our wealth, and our muscle will determine the character of the new century. If we do not lead, then no one else will. If we are unwilling to tackle the peacekeeping mission, then the peace will not be kept.

There are those, too, who criticize an evolutionary transformation because they are caught in the spell of seductive new technologies. Americans have always been fascinated by such developments. We pioneered the modern age through invention and ingenuity. Give us a problem, we say, and we will fix it with a machine. Very often we do. But not always.

Defense is a hard, exacting task. Many disappointments occur along the way. You know from your own experience that everything works fine, and then the computer goes down. Sometimes it is not so easy to bring it back up. What we must avoid at all costs is reliance on what soldiers call the "silver bullet"—the idea that technological magic will fix it all around. We went down that road nearly two decades ago with what some called Star Wars, the quest for an effective missile defense. I hope some day we can deploy one that works. But so far, despite spending over $75 billion, we have not found one, and we cannot plan our security around one. Nor can we risk antagonizing Russia and China and possibly driving them into a military alliance, or alienating our European allies, by deploying a system that does not even work.

I am therefore proceeding carefully with what some have called a revolution in military affairs. We are going to adapt our forces as need be, but we are not going to gamble our future security on unproven technologies, no matter how exciting they appear. To put it bluntly, radical overhauls are neither necessary, desirable, nor possible.

Finally, we must not accept the views of those who play down the dangers we face and would, in the name of other budget priorities, make major reductions in military spending. There is simply no way for the United States to combat terrorism, meet threats from evil regimes in Asia and the Middle East, keep forces deployed in Europe, and carry out peacekeeping missions, with a force smaller than the one I propose. Just consider the risk to our interests. If confronted by a crisis in more than one region, we would have to make an agonizing choice: Which is most important, our security in Asia, in Europe, or in the Middle East? The American people would never forgive a president for such a lack of foresight or preparation. A safer rule is this: do not reduce the forces until after the risks are reduced. I have weighed our security risks carefully and consider this force the minimum needed to undertake all the tasks that support our foreign policy. This smaller force has limits, but they are well within the acceptable range of risks for our strategy.

The changes I propose will not give us a larger force than we field today but one that is more formidable and effective. We have agreed with the Russians to reduce our strategic nuclear forces to between 1,700 and 2,200 warheads. In this day and age, there is no need to keep an expensive and overly large nuclear arsenal when a smaller and more efficient one will achieve the same overall level of deterence. The United States will also lead the way in nonproliferation efforts as well as arms-control agreements, particularly the Comprehensive Test Ban Treaty—which I will ask Congress to ratify—in further efforts to reduce the nuclear powers' dependence on large arsenals. As the entire active force drops from 1.45 million personnel to 1.3 million by 2003, the Army and Air Force will lose some troops, but they will keep their combat power. Changes in technology, organization, and doctrine will allow smaller, lighter units to be just as lethal on the battlefield as were the larger units of the past. The Navy will retain a 12-carrier force, the size needed to extend our global presence and fighting power. The United States will also maintain its forward deployments in Europe, Asia, and the Persian Gulf. Smaller reserve forces will be focused primarily on defending the homeland and providing some support to active-duty troops during overseas deployments. We will increase spending on new weapons and on innovation, and we will continue to conduct vigorous research and development on projects such as a national missile defense. But for the time being, we will not deploy a missile defense.

In the meantime, I have asked the secretary of defense to implement several concepts that will further tailor our military to the challenges of the future. These concepts are designed to:

- Ensure that the Pentagon takes advantage of changing business practices to streamline its administrative procedures and organizational structure;

- Train our troops to be equally proficient at peacekeeping and combat operations;

- Prepare some military units specifically for peacekeeping duties;

- Implement new readiness and rotational policies to alleviate some of the strain on frequently deployed units;

- Reduce the overseas U.S. presence slightly without upsetting the balance of power in a particular region or America's leadership role in its alliances; and

- Reform our military compensation system and quality of life programs to increase recruitment and retention.

STEADY AS WE GO

Members of Congress, the evolutionary defense plan I have put before you prepares us for the potential dangers ahead. It avoids the serious blunder of abandoning our peacekeeping responsibilities. And it brings a sharper focus to our overall defense plan by shifting the emphasis from large and expensive combat forces kept at hair-trigger readiness to research and procurement for the future. We are not going to make the mistake of spending too much where we are already strong enough, risking too much on emerging technologies, or abandoning essential missions. The current defense budget will increase only to keep pace with inflation.

As we look forward, the motto "steady as we go" is the most efficient choice in defense policy. In the past, more often than not, the United States has pursued a less wise course: that of arming suddenly to meet a crisis and then disarming quickly once the crisis has passed. This is a wasteful and costly way to run our national defense. It deprives our peacetime diplomacy of leverage and invites trouble from our adversaries. We simply cannot afford to do business that way any longer.

Since the end of the Cold War, by contrast, we have sought to avoid such a "feast or famine" defense policy. The uncertainties are too large and, as recent events have shown, the world still too unsettled for the United States to abandon its leadership role or the military power behind it. We have therefore reduced our military from the size necessary to fight the Cold War, but we have kept it at the size necessary to sustain our international leadership. After a decade of declining spending, we have now increased our defense budget to an appropriate level.

What I ask of you tonight is simply support for staying the course. This is no small thing. A properly focused, steady-as-you-go, more efficient defense policy requires just as much energy and imagination as any alternative. And persistence is a test of our character and our wisdom. We know from our own lives that finding the right path is half the job; the other half is to keep at it. Let it be said, therefore, of this generation of Americans that after winning the Cold War, we knew how to win the peace. Let us be sure that our armed forces continue forever to be the best-equipped, most highly trained, and most wisely led force in the world.

SPEECH FOUR: A COOPERATIVE DEFENSE

A plan to refocus our overly large and expensive Cold War military on cooperative responses to the current challenges of global security, such as terrorists with global reach and failed states such as Kosovo, Bosnia, and Macedonia—while reducing overall military spending by 15 to 20 percent.

Members of Congress and My Fellow Americans:

Thank you for welcoming me to Capitol Hill this evening. I have decided to speak directly to this special joint session of Congress because we face important decisions that will affect our national security far into the future. Since the end of the Cold War, we have supported reduced but still very large and expensive armed forces. We have hedged against threats and uncertainties not only to protect our interests but also to shape the emerging international order. But the world has changed, the risks have changed with it, and we need to redesign our defense policy to accord with the new realities.

Despite having lived through more than a decade since the end of the Cold War, we still find it difficult to shed the mindsets, habits, vocabularies, and policies born of nearly a half-century of unrelenting state-to-state confrontation. For much of that time, the fate of civilization arguably hung in the balance. And today, we continue to think in terms of us-versus-them rather than cooperative regimes of mutual security; of deterrence rather than assurance; and of imagined or exaggerated threats rather than diplomatic and economic initiatives designed to improve long-standing relationships.

Let me be more specific. The dangers we face today come less from a potential international rival, such as Russia or China, and more from failing states, such as Rwanda and the former Yugoslavia, and transnational terrorist groups. If allowed to fester, the problems in these failing states will sooner or later undermine the prospects for general peace and prosperity, particularly if terrorists find a safe haven in one of them, as al Qaeda did in Afghanistan. In addition, global problems such as environmental threats, changing demographics, refugees, and scarce resources affect our security as much as or more than any adversarial army. The solution for all these problems cannot only be "made in America" but must involve the community of nations. The United States, as the preeminent power in the world today, must take the initiative to support such cooperative action because it is the most effective way to deal with these issues. In doing so, we will also be drawing together former adversaries and giving them an increased stake in international stability.

Such an approach requires an American military force and a defense strategy in accord with the new realities. I am therefore proposing a three-point plan in which we will:

- Reform U.S. forces to make them more effective at counter terrorism, homeland defense, peacekeeping, and small- and medium-scale interventions.

- Take the initiative to build international institutions and alliances in a new, cooperative effort that rallies America's allies and friends to deal with these common problems. The coalition we assembled to wage the war in Afghanistan is a prime example of the fruits of such efforts. This leadership—which will include leading the way in new arms-control initiatives aimed at reducing nuclear arsenals and other weapons of mass destruction, as well as continued reliance on deterrence rather than on developing and deploying an expensive and destabilizing national missile defense system—should halt the current backlash against American unilateralism.

- Retain the capability for a swift military expansion in case of emergency, while eliminating unnecessary forces and structures.

This plan will sharply reduce American defense expenditures and strengthen our economy. But that is not the best reason to do it. The main purpose of our defense policy is, and always must be, to strengthen our security.

[78]

Our defense planning begins with the definition of our interests and the threats to them. The American people know that a secure and peaceful world is fundamental to our freedom and prosperity in this era of globalization. America has forged important trade links with Europe, Asia, the Middle East, and our neighbors in the Americas. These ties are still growing and form part of our broadening definition of national security, which places increasing emphasis on a robust economy rather than on the mere accumulation of arms. The financial crises in Asia, Russia, Turkey, Brazil, and Argentina have shown us how troubles in global markets overseas can affect our security and prosperity.

Despite the inherent risks, we Americans should welcome this trend of economic integration because it promises a world less afflicted by military competition. But such a world can emerge only when nations feel secure and stability is assured. There are more plowshares today than there used to be, yet as we saw on September 11, there are still plenty of swords, and we face a range of uncertainties that demands a strong defense.

NEW CHALLENGES

Since the end of the Cold War, our military strategists have been focused on several problems, and I want to report on our progress.

Reducing the Nuclear Threat
Now that the Cold War has ended, we no longer have to fear an apocalyptic nuclear war. But huge arsenals still exist. Violent and irresponsible leaders might yet acquire weapons of mass destruction—nuclear, biological, or chemical—and use them against the United States. We have therefore been working through arms-control initiatives and sanctions against violators to reduce this danger. And, as you will hear tonight, I propose that we redouble our efforts in this most important task and take the lead in reducing nuclear arsenals even further.

Cooperating with Former Adversaries

Our Russian counterparts are going through wrenching political and economic change. Working through NATO, the International Monetary Fund, and our own aid programs, we have attempted to foster a more cooperative and democratic Russia. We have managed to sustain a cooperative relationship with Moscow while leading the way to NATO enlargement in order to solidify the new democracies of central Europe. These achievements have permitted large reductions in the U.S. forces deployed in Europe.

Turning to Asia, U.S. policy is to foster constructive relations with China, the world's most populous nation, which is also engaged in a profound transformation. We have also worked with Japan and others to resolve conflicts; when necessary, we have reminded the region of our interest in free passage, free trade, and human rights. As in Europe, this policy has allowed for a smaller but still substantial American military presence.

Containing Leaders of So-Called Rogue or Evil States

American troops are most at risk today on the Korean Peninsula, where a North Korean regime shaken by economic failure still threatens our South Korean ally with a huge military force. Nonetheless, we have made some headway in controlling North Korea's attempt to build nuclear weapons and in bringing about peace talks with South Korea. Moreover, we have helped South Korea become a capable democratic ally, with armed forces that are today more than a match for those of the north.

In the Persian Gulf, U.S. troops, ships, and aircraft are actively patrolling no-fly zones and helping to enforce sanctions against Iraq, which no longer allows weapons inspections by U.N. monitors. The peace of the gulf region, however, is also endangered by Iran, a supporter of terrorism and again a state seeking nuclear and other weapons of mass destruction and the means to deliver them. Under its new, democratically elected president, Iran has been making peaceful overtures to the United States that are bearing fruit. Nonetheless, we have been working with local allies and the United Nations to contain both Iraq and Iran, and as a result, neither has been able to harm our interests significantly since the

Persian Gulf War. In fact, Iran even furnished us with some help in the war in Afghanistan.

Stabilizing Failed States

Revolutions in communications, the global economy, the spread of ideas, and the end of ideologies are remaking the face of our world. We have seen huge movements of peoples—some as refugees, others as immigrants—all seeking a better life. But not every nation has been able to deal with these changes successfully. Some states have failed, their societies disintegrating into savage civil wars. Old doctrines of racial and ethnic hatred have acquired new life through "ethnic cleansing" and other actions repugnant to our values. We have worked with the United Nations, NATO, and other forums of international cooperation to stabilize such situations in places like Cambodia, Haiti, Bosnia, Rwanda, Kosovo, Macedonia, Sierra Leone, and East Timor—and we have had mixed success.

National security in the era of globalization is about much more than guarding the Fulda Gap in Germany against an invasion from the Warsaw Pact countries or deterring potential adversaries with an overwhelming nuclear force. Today, national security is also about economic relations with allies and former adversaries, human rights in the developing world, the mounting environmental challenges in industrial states, and stability in many different areas affected by the end of Cold War political structures. If the international community does not handle these problems, citizens will turn increasingly to terrorism.

As we have dealt with these issues, we have become more and more aware of one fact: we need a broad and flexible military power, but one very different from what we had before. Since the end of the Cold War, defense policy has been driven by the desire to reduce the budget in line with both the reduced threat and our domestic priorities, giving us a military that has shrunk by one-third. Nevertheless, our force is still dominated by an obsolete nuclear and conventional structure, and it is still designed to counter the least likely threat: a Soviet-style challenge. As a result, the United States is burdened with a very expensive but misdirected military prepared for large-scale warfare rather than the challenges and operations that American forces have faced with increasing strain. In Afghanistan, it was the leadership of our special forces, which consume less than one percent of the defense budget, that enabled us to defeat the Taliban so quickly and with so few casualties.

This trend should not and cannot continue. The essence of government is choice. Despite our great power, the United States cannot meet every contingency by itself. The vain attempt to do so only stretches our resources and leaves us with inadequate forces. Instead, we must hedge against uncertainties while retaining enough capability for rapid response in the case of a clear and present danger.

An effective defense policy for our times, therefore, begins with a choice. Which threats are receding, soon to be relegated to history books? Which challenges are approaching, for which we should prepare ourselves? What do we hedge against, and how do we do it?

As the Cold War fades from our memories, the answers to these questions have become clearer. Today and for the foreseeable future, we can be assured that:

- The Soviet-style threat is gone. The United States has no global rivals, and none will emerge for a decade or more. There are those who would paint China as a new strategic competitor of the United States, but in reality, we are threatened more by China's weakness than its strength. As evidence of the new era, Russia and China have provided invaluable support to us in the war against the Taliban.

- The threat from the so-called rogue or evil states is decreasing. Iraq is crippled. North Korea is failing. Neither can expect aid from a superpower; their economies are disasters; and their regimes must change, for it is not the people of Iraq and North Korea who are a threat but their incompetent rulers. As we demonstrated in Operation Desert Storm, the Iraqi military was no match for America's capabilities. We are even further ahead of these states now, and the gap is still widening.

- The nuclear threat, aside from the danger of terrorism and pro-liferation, is substantially diminished. The issue should be not whether the reduction in nuclear arsenals will continue, but how quickly the major powers can reduce them. We will diminish the nuclear threat even more by leading the effort to disarm even further and increasing spending on such cooperative threat reduction programs as Nunn-Lugar. Moreover, even the dangers of weapons proliferation and terrorism are on a much different scale than that of the nuclear standoff of yesteryear.

The real challenges we face are of a different order. The problems of failed states, civil wars, and refugees originate within states but become most dangerous when they cross borders or even dissolve them. You know some of the names: Afghanistan. Somalia. Haiti. Rwanda. Bosnia. Kosovo. East Timor. Macedonia. No region of the world has been spared.

We must not underestimate the impact of this problem. Like a spreading virus, the ideologies, passions, and refugees let loose by such failed states can destabilize a region or the entire world. And although we and our allies might like to ignore or downplay the matter, the cumulative impact of our inaction will eventually undermine our own safety, a fact dramatically made clear on September 11. Crimes are being committed, and criminals take note of our reaction.

Let us be honest with ourselves. We have had a very mixed record thus far in dealing with such crises, partly because we have been unprepared for them. Peacekeeping and stability operations are not what America planned to do when we designed our armed forces during the Cold War. Our soldiers, sailors, marines, and airmen are trained to fight wars, not win the peace. They train to find the enemy, seize the strategic ground, advance, and defeat the adversary. Peacekeeping is not like that at all.

The training problem presents its own challenge to our military professionalism, while the United States faces a special dilemma in dealing with peacekeeping operations.

The dilemma is this: American involvement, especially with our troops, may go beyond our immediate interests. We cannot be the policeman of the world, summoned whenever anything goes wrong anywhere. But American refusal to get involved often leads to the absence of action by other members of the international community, as demonstrated in Afghanistan in 1989. This inaction may eventually create a threat to our interests when a situation spirals out of control. We cannot simply abdicate our leadership when it comes to international order.

There is only one way to police the world without America becoming the policeman. We must have effective U.S. military forces acting primarily in conjunction with other nations and international institutions so that burdens and risks are shared and every crisis does not become primarily an American responsibility. To achieve this goal, we must increasingly rely on diplomacy, humanitarian aid, and preventive actions to resolve problems before they become armed conflicts and to work through multilateral approaches to solve conflicts when they occur.

A THREE-POINT PLAN

I am proposing tonight a three-point plan that reshapes our forces to deal with both the decreased need for large deterrent forces and the increased need for a multilateral effort that assures international stability. The strategy outlined by this plan will transform our military into an institution uniquely suited to deal with the new problems of the post–Cold War world and will at the same time leave us with an effective residual capability for conventional military action.

1. Rebalance Our Forces to Meet Today's Spectrum of Threats.
We will gear a larger proportion of our military toward conducting counterterrorism operations, small- and medium-scale interventions, and peacekeeping or stability operations. We should equip such forces with the latest technology for their missions, taking advantage of the revolutions in stealth, long-range strike capability, and communications. And we must ensure that these forces can be deployed swiftly.

We will also strengthen our military capabilities—both conventional and special—especially those designed to improve cooperation with the militaries of other nations. These changes include:

- An emphasis on long-range precision munitions that will reduce the danger to our close-combat units and make coalition and alliance forces more effective.

- Recognition of the importance of information warfare, including surveillance and reconnaissance systems, and improved communications.

- A greater role for increased numbers of special operations units able to act in conjunction with those of our allies.

- A renewed emphasis on homeland defense.

2. Create More Effective International Security Mechanisms.
Much of American foreign policy has been designed to establish effective international organizations that transform national competition into cooperative action. Through NATO in Europe and the U.S.-Japan security alliance in Asia, we have created communities of common interest where the commonly agreed-upon rules are actually followed. As we have seen, however, the international community still lacks a practical security design that would combine diplomatic efforts with an effective international military force.

The United States alone, as I have said earlier, cannot and should not deal with these challenges unilaterally. That leaves two choices in dealing with terrorists, the failed states, and other potential aggressors of the 21st century: the United Nations or regional allies. Our initial post–Cold War effort to vest some military responsibilities in the United Nations may have been premature, but it was not wrong. The forward-looking men and women who established the U.N. Security Council in 1945 foresaw the organization's need to have forces at its disposal.

No less a figure than Winston Churchill, in the forgotten part of his "Iron Curtain" speech, repeated his support for such a U.N. force, with dedicated national units on which to draw. I will therefore suggest to the U.N. Security Council and secretary-general that this subject again be put on the agenda. The United Nations need not immediately acquire a permanent standing force under its control, but we should work toward that goal. In the interim, the organization should have more reliable access to well-trained and well-equipped international forces in times of crisis. In this way, we might be able to avoid disasters like those that occurred in Afghanistan in 1989, Rwanda in 1994, or Sierra Leone in 2000.

The United Nations, however, is not the only institution that can deal with the problem of international instability. America is blessed with strong allies and numerous friends. Together, we have common interests in stabilizing the international order. Some of our allies have powerful (if limited) military forces, and others are prepared to offer economic assistance. We already have experience with allied cooperation in Bosnia, Kosovo, and Afghanistan.

The time has come, therefore, to make these arrangements more permanent. Our initial proposal will be to establish permanent rapid-reaction units drawn from a coalition of those powers able and willing to cooperate. In these units, as in the overall planning, there should be a division of labor, each party doing what it does best. Militarily, this will mean in most cases the deployment of unique American assets, such as logistics, airlift, special forces, and tactical aircraft, rather than major American combat units—although we should be prepared to deploy the latter in case of emergency. This is what was done in Somalia in late 1992 on an ad hoc basis, as the United States led 26 other nations in an improvised coalition to relieve the horrible famine there. The key to success now is to find the degree to which we can institutionalize that sort of cooperation.

Too often in the past, American defense planning has been conducted in a vacuum, without fully recognizing the like-minded states that become our partners in almost any military operation. Today, the question is not whether a mission will be unilateral or multilateral, but what kind of multilateral operation we will choose to conduct. I am convinced that we do not yet take full advantage of our long-term alliances and our short-term partners who share many of our security concerns. We must integrate more fully the efforts of our allies into this new cooperative scheme. Doing so will include encouraging allies to maintain vigorous defenses, as many have slashed their defense budgets or disarmed too soon. For our part, we must also let allies lead in the smaller collective security missions, especially when they have greater interests at stake. I am particularly encouraged by the European Union's willingness to establish a military force of 50,000 troops to deal with situations like the Balkans conflicts. The United States need not lead everywhere and in every cause to maintain its status as a world leader. And we will certainly not prevail in the war against terrorism without help from other nations.

3. Restructure Our Forces.

The retirement of our current Cold War structure, which is wasteful and not up to the job, is long overdue. Over the next five years, we will therefore retire 30 percent of the current active force. This smaller military will rely heavily on the reserves in case of emergency. The new defense policy places greater emphasis on reserve air power, combat support, and combat-service support functions—all areas in which reserve forces have excelled. Resources will be redirected to ensure that the National Guard can carry out the homeland security mission. These moves do not come without cost, and I will tell you tonight that our military will be less able to respond to large challenges as quickly as it has in the past. However, this risk is very low and well worth taking. It is simply a waste of money and other resources to keep a huge military force on hair-trigger readiness for the conflicts of the last century.

A critical part of our plan will also be to hedge against new threats. New technologies and systems will be developed and tested as prototypes, but they need not be manufactured in quantity unless the threat warrants it. As part of this approach, I favor research into ballistic missile defenses as a hedge but not deploying it any time soon. We will certainly not take any action that might spark a nuclear arms race in Asia, nor will we decouple our security from that of our NATO allies.

Clearly, this much smaller and more suitable force carries with it dramatic changes in the military budget. Active-duty forces will be reduced from the current 1.45 million people to about 1 million.

There will be just over 700,000 personnel in reserves. Our nuclear warheads will be reduced considerably from their present level of 6,000 to below 1,000. The Pentagon will procure upgraded versions of the current generation of existing systems, which are the best in the world. For example, the Air Force will purchase the F-16 Block 60 at a cost of $30 million rather than the F-22 for more than $225 million.

All in all, we will be trimming our military costs from 3.5 percent of GDP and 16 percent of the federal budget to about 2 percent and 10 percent, respectively, over a five-year period. If all our efficiency measures are realized, these costs will translate into annual defense expenditures of about $300 billion a year after 2005, substantially below the current level of $400 billion. The procurement part of the budget will decline from $60 billion to $50 billion, but research and development will increase slightly to $40 billion, and the pay of our military men and women will rise substantially.

This new force will result in changes in military organization and tactics. I have therefore directed the secretary of defense to make the following alterations:

- Combine our research on ballistic missile defense with that of other nations, including Russia, to advance the common cause.

- Change the current unit structures of the Army and Marine Corps to give us similar effectiveness with fewer personnel.

- Consolidate the existing industrial base and change the remaining portion to reflect quality research and experimentation but not expensive procurement.

- Create specialized units in both the active force and the reserves for peacekeeping and humanitarian relief operations.

- Retrain much of the reserve forces and some active forces to specialize in homeland defense, especially information warfare, counterterrorism, and protection against weapons of mass destruction.

THE REAL ISSUES

Let no one fear that these changes will leave us with a weak military. At the end of it all, we will have a conventional force some 30 percent smaller across the board but more than adequate for the types of challenges we will face in today's world, and we will still be spending more on defense than all of our potential adversaries combined. Moreover, despite some recent cutbacks, our allies are also spending significant sums on defense. For example, our European allies spend more on defense than Russia, Japan outspends China, Israel outspends Iraq, and South Korea outspends North Korea. We will continue to keep some forces forward-deployed in both Asia and Europe, but in much reduced numbers and at a lower cost. If we have to fight a major conflict in either of these theaters, which I do not expect will happen, we will reinforce our small forward-deployed forces with active and reserve forces sent from the United States. Money saved from closing bases both overseas and in the United States will be used to increase our strategic airlift capability, replacing large forward-based troops with more mobile units that can be flown to crisis areas with little notice.

Our expensive and largely redundant nuclear force will be reduced immediately to no more than 1,000 warheads. I am convinced, however, that we can safely afford to reduce much further, and I have asked the National Security Council to see how much more we can cut our nuclear arsenal and to explore other initiatives such as taking most of our nuclear forces off hair-trigger alert status while asking the other nuclear powers to follow suit. I will personally ask the Senate to take up the Comprehensive Test Ban Treaty again as well as to ratify the Biological Weapons Protocol, the Small Arms Control Pact, the Ottawa Treaty banning land mines, and the Rome Treaty establishing the International Criminal Court. In this day and age, we must question past concepts of deterrence predicated on large nuclear arsenals. That is the sort of old thinking we can now safely challenge—a challenge for which we will reap many rewards.

In addition, we will build on the 1967 Outer Space Treaty to prevent the militarization of space. The last thing this nation and the world need is an arms race in space. Such an arms race would make the danger of the Cold War–era nuclear arms race seem trivial. Finally, we will continue to abide by our agreement with Moscow to help reduce Russia's vast and ill-guarded stockpile of weapons-grade plutonium. The United States will enjoy a much greater return in real security terms from spending $8 billion over ten years on this initiative rather than $8 billion a year on national missile defense.

My fellow Americans, I can think of few periods in our history when greater changes were demanded of our armed forces than those I am proposing. Some will see in this program a dangerous disarmament. They are wrong. In fact, the "cooperative defense" I have discussed with you is a program for arming America with the forces we need to meet the challenges of the new age. Even with these changes, the United States will still possess the most powerful standing military on earth by a substantial margin and, together with its allies, will account for 75 percent of the world's military expenditures. We will certainly be able to defend the continental United States, its territories overseas, and the areas vital to our national interest. We will also be better able to respond to those challenges that are most important in this era of globalization.

Today's threat, I repeat, is not the sudden reappearance of a Soviet-style attack. It is not the breakout of a rogue regime. It is not a superpower nuclear arms race. These dangers are largely in the past. By keeping an outdated and outsized military against such receding dangers, we only weaken ourselves in dealing with the real problems, whether they are terrorists or failed states. And instead of meeting those challenges, we are wasting untold sums on the wrong forces for the wrong occasions. It is a mistake to believe that spending money alone will guarantee our safety. There is no such thing as deterrence by appropriation.

The United States must therefore reequip, retrain, and reorganize its forces to deal with the real issues. We must also revive and redouble our efforts to recruit international cooperation to deal with security problems of common interest. We will not be able to win the war against terrorism without help from the international community. There are tradeoffs, naturally. The United States will no longer be able to unilaterally send large military forces to several crises at once and will depend greatly on preventive diplomacy and allied support to assist in those instances. In the unlikely event of a significant conflict, it will take time to mobilize the reserves in order to reinforce our smaller active forces. These are risks, however, that are well worth taking. I am confident that with your support, the Americans who volunteer to protect us all through military service will master these new challenges with the same "can do" enthusiasm we have come to expect of them.

The military has a good term that sums up the idea behind a cooperative defense: a "force multiplier." Our armed services, combined with those of our allies abroad, using international mechanisms, will multiply the successes of our efforts to secure the blessings of peace and freedom. The methods will be different from those of the past, but the result will be the same: a safer future for America and, through cooperation in the common interest, for the rest of the world as well.

FIGURES

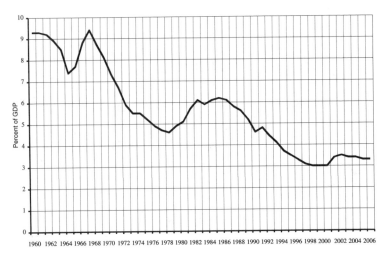

Figure 1. Defense Spending as a Share of GDP, 1960–2007

SOURCE: Office of Management and Budget, National Defense Budget Estimates for FY2003, Historical Tables, February 2002.

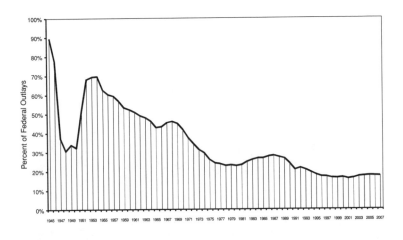

Figure 2. Defense Spending as a Share of Federal Outlays, 1945–2007

SOURCE: Office of Management and Budget, National Defense Budget Estimates for FY2003, Historical Tables, February 2002.

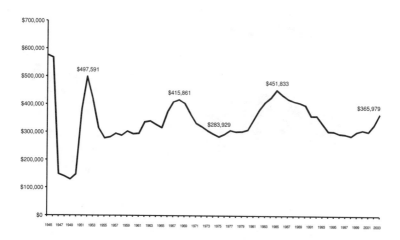

Figure 3. DoD Annual Budget Authority, 1945–2003
(In millions of FY2002 constant dollars)

SOURCE: Office of Management and Budget, National Defense Budget Estimates for FY2003, February 2002.

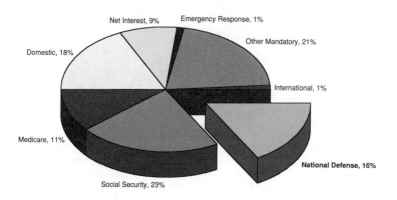

Figure 4. Federal Budget Requests, FY2003

SOURCE: Center for Strategic Budgetary Assessments, February 2002. Based on Office of Management and Budget data.

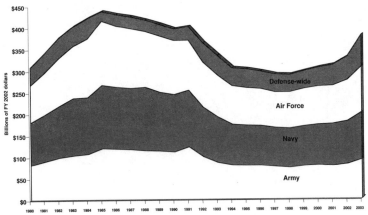

Figure 5. DoD Budget by Service, 1980-2003

SOURCE: *Department of Defense Budget for FY2003.* Includes funding for Desert Shield/Desert Storm; excludes allied Gulf War contributions.

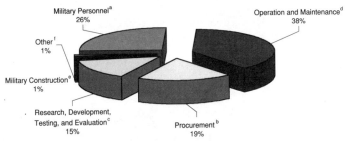

Figure 6. Makeup of DoD Budget, FY2003

SOURCE: Office of Management and Budget, FY2003. Based on data from the Department of Defense, FY2003.

a. "Operation and Maintenance" (O&M) includes spending on fuel, spare parts, and overhauls of military equipment. O&M also includes spending on such items as health care, management (by, for example, the Office of the Secretary of Defense, the Joint Staff, and service staffs at headquarters), environmental programs (e.g., pollution prevention and environmental restoration), real property maintenance (e.g., the maintenance and repair of buildings, roadways, and runways), base operating support (e.g., child care and family support), and communications (e.g., telephone systems and computer infrastructure).

b. "Military Personnel" includes spending on salaries and benefits.

c. "Procurement" includes purchases of new equipment and paying for major modifications of existing systems.

d. "Research, Development, Testing, and Evaluation" covers the costs of development and testing new systems and subsystems.

e. "Military Construction" pays for building new facilities and support structures for military installations.

f. "Other" includes spending on family housing and management of working capital revolving funds.